Hunting Halifax

In Search of History,
Mystery and Murder

Steven Edwin Laffoley

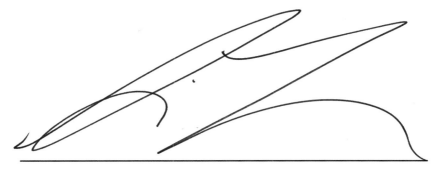

Pottersfield Press, Lawrencetown Beach, Nova Scotia, Canada

Library and Archives Canada Cataloguing in Publication

Library and Archives Canada Cataloguing in Publication

Laffoley, Steven Edwin
    Hunting Halifax : in search of history, mystery and murder / Steven Edwin Laffoley.

ISBN 978-1-895900-93-4

1. Laffoley, Steven Edwin – Anecdotes. 1. Halifax (N.S.) – Anecdotes.
2. Halifax (N.S.) – History. I. Title.

FC2346.4.L35 2007   971.6'225   C2007-904661-4

Cover design by Gail LeBlanc

Pottersfield Press acknowledges the financial support of the Government of Canada through the Book Publishing Industry Development Program for our publishing activities. We also acknowledge the ongoing support of the Canada Council for the Arts, which last year invested $20.1 million in writing and publishing throughout Canada. We also thank the Province of Nova Scotia for its support through the Department of Tourism, Culture and Heritage.

Pottersfield Press
83 Leslie Road
East Lawrencetown, Nova Scotia, Canada, B2Z 1P8
Website: www.pottersfieldpress.com
To order phone toll-free 1-800-NIMBUS9 (1-800-646-2879)

Printed in Canada

For Bernice and Emma

Acknowledgements

Many thanks to the following who helped make this book happen: Lesley Choyce, Julia Swan, and Peggy Amirault for their enthusiasm, advice, and assistance; and David Wiggin and Deborah Goodfellow for their open ears and unqualified encouragement.

Contents

Barrack Street
(An Old Sailor's Ballad)

You sailors all, come lend an ear, come listen to my song.
A trick of late was played on me, it won't detain you long.
I came from sea the other day, a girl I chanced to meet,
"My friends will be expecting me to a dance on Barrack Street."

I said, "My pretty one, I cannot dance too well,
Besides, I am to Windsor bound, where all my friends do dwell.
I've been to sea these last two years, I've saved up £30,
My friends will be expecting me this night in Windsor town."

At eight o'clock that evening the drinking did begin,
And when all hands had got their fill the dancing did begin.
Me and my love danced all around unto a merry tune,
When she says, "Dear, we will retire to a chamber all alone."

The dancing being over, to bed we did repair,
And there I fell fast asleep, the truth I will declare,
My darling with my £30, gold watch and chain had fled,
And left me here, poor Jack alone, left naked in the bed.

I looked all around me, nothing could I spy
But a woman's shirt and apron upon the bed did lie.
I wrung my hands and tore my hair, crying "What shall I do?"
Fare you well, sweet Windsor town, I'm sure I'll ne'er see you.

Everything being silent, and the hour but twelve o'clock,
I put on my shirt and apron and steered for Cronan's dock,
And when I did get on board the sailors all did say,
"I think, old chap, you've had a duck since you have been away."

"Is those the new spring fashions which have lately come on shore?
Where is the shop you bought them at, do you think there's any more?"
The captain, he says, "Jack, I thought you were to Windsor bound,
You might have got a better suit than that for £30."

"I might have got a better suit if I'd had a chance.
I met a girl in Water Street. She asked me to a dance.
I danced my own destruction; I'm stripped from head to feet,
I'll take my oath I'll go no more to a dance on Barrack Street."

Come, all you young sailor lads, a warning take by me,
Be sure and choose your company
When you go on a spree;

Be sure keep out of Barrack Street, or else you'll rue the day,
With a woman's shirt and apron they'll rig you out for sea.

(Helen Creighton, *Songs and Ballads from Nova Scotia*)

Preface

The Ghosts

I believe in ghosts – sort of.

Consider:

We are each shaped by the past, by the stories we tell ourselves and the stories we tell our children. But more than this, we are, in a real sense, haunted by the past. It floats like pollen in the air we breathe and hides like fibre in the food we eat. It vibrates, imperceptibly, in every molecule and every atom that permeates our blood and our bone, our sentience and our soul. The past makes us human, shaping us unconsciously and relentlessly, prefacing and explaining our understanding of self and place. It is our great collective story, nearly 200,000 years old now, which began with our genetic Eve who once walked slowly and deliberately along an ancient rock formation in Omo Kibish, Ethiopia. That Eve was our first ghost, her actions the first vibrations of our collective story.

This story is an echo of that first vibration. It's about the past, and about ghosts – sort of. Certainly, it starts as good ghost stories do, in an old city cemetery, where not long ago, I found myself lying recumbent among the falling leaves of autumn. Why was I lying in an old cemetery, recumbent among the falling leaves of autumn? Well, you'll just have to read on, I guess. But for now, let's just say that, as a consequence of being in that old cemetery, I found myself wondering about a black hole in local history, a stretch between 1843 and 1857 when a generation of a city's citizens lived between the closing of the first and oldest city graveyard to the construction, in that same spot, some fifteen years later, of a conspicuously misplaced brownstone monument to the great Crimean War.

Why did I wonder about this? Well, for two reasons – both relatively rational. Firstly, Haligonians – the name of those lucky souls who live in Halifax, Nova Scotia, the city in which the old cemetery is located – seemed to know, on the whole, a good deal about their city's distant past, about its founding in 1749 and about its role in the American Revolution and the Revolution's popular sequel, the War of 1812. So too, these Haligonians seemed to know, on the whole, a fair bit about their post-1860 history: Canadian Confederation, the Halifax Explosion, World Wars I and II, and the Cold War. Certainly, as any Haligonian would tell you, the ghosts of 1749, 1812, 1867, 1917, and 1945 all tangibly haunt Halifax in the city's treasured tales and storied structures. But that day, lying recumbent in the cemetery, I wondered: was it possible that the ghosts of, say, 1853 still haunted us in ways we couldn't quite perceive?

The second relatively rational reason I wondered about this black hole in history was this: the years between 1843 and 1857 marked not only the closing of the city's oldest cemetery and the construction of the strangely juxtaposed Crimean War monument, but it also corresponded, more or less, with one of the great turning points in modern history: the social, cultural, and economic shift – tectonic in proportion – from an agricultural age to an industrial age. This local historic dead zone in Halifax interested me, in part, because Haligonians live today in a comparable period in their history: a social, cultural, economic shift – also tectonic in proportion – from an industrial age to a digital age. What lessons, I considered, might this black hole in history have to teach us?

So, some months later, armed with a black Hilroy notebook and a mechanical pencil, I made my way to the Nova Scotia Archives, where I pored over reels and reels of old Halifax newspapers – the

Novascotian, *The Halifax Herald*, and *The Daily Sun* among others. With the information I gathered from these newspapers, I filled my notebook with the myriad mundane details of the time – the dry dates and the atomized events of the distant past. Yet the more I investigated, the more this period seemed an eventless, even ghostless, history lesson. No striking, compelling tales to fire the imagination. No ghosts of 1853 to tangibly haunt the present. After a few weeks of this, I was about ready to give up.

Then came the surprise.

One humid afternoon, while sitting in a dark corner of the Archives, spinning through yet another reel of the *Halifax Morning Chronicle*, I randomly stopped on a page from September 10, 1853. On it, I read warehouse advertisements for leather goods, market advertisements for local meats, and the shipping news about the comings and goings in the harbour. And just before I turned the lever to forward the page, I read this:

Supposed Murder of a Sailor

> One of the crew of H.M.S. Cumberland, named Alexander Allen, was discovered dead, or nearly so, on the steps leading to the Waterloo Tavern, Barrack Street, on Thursday morning shortly after midnight. When picked up his head was horribly wounded. A Coroner's Inquest is now investigating the case. The Jury is composed of six men-of-war's men and six civilians. The Inquest sat on Thursday and yesterday until dark, and adjourned over last night until this morning at 10 o'clock. Of course we make no further remarks until the Verdict is returned. Meanwhile we are noting the proceedings of this most mysterious affair, the particulars of which shall be duly chronicled for the information of our numerous readers.

I was hooked.

Over the next hour, I rifled through other reels of microfiche and found two more mentions of the mystery in two different newspapers. Then, returning to the stacks, I rummaged through the shelves and unearthed more microfiche reels on which I found the coroner's inquest report: the rough sketch details and witness testimony of what happened the night of the "supposed murder," all wonderfully contradictory and strikingly emotional. It was then that I realized I'd found, hidden among the mountains of dry day-to-day facts, the voices of real people.

That is, I found my ghosts.

And I was riveted.

Over the next few days, I uncovered testimony from the murder trial where witnesses took the stand and told their tales; where lawyers made their arguments, and judges made their rulings; and where the assembled courtroom crowd murmured and gasped and laughed. Soon, a distinctive cast of characters emerged, and with it, so too did the story of a city in a period of dramatic change.

My tale, it seemed, was at last taking shape – but then came a final twist.

One morning, while walking the street where the "supposed murder" occurred, I casually wondered if any physical evidence of the crime might still exist. The idea intrigued me. So, like a time-travelling detective, I started poking about the streets, the alleys, and the taverns of present-day Halifax looking for century-and-a-half-old clues. And that's how this book came to be: these three tales playfully intertwining – history, mystery, and murder.

Who could ask for more?

Oh, and for the record, the events described, and the details discussed, and even the words spoken are all real – or, at least, all reasonable, well-founded reconstructions, drawn from the testimony of witnesses and firsthand observations. I like to think of it this way: as author James Ellroy once said of a book, "The novel was a willful distortion in the service of human truth." The facts that follow are fleshed out from time to time with reasonable surmise. Any "willful distortions" are offered, as Ellroy noted, "in the service of human truth."

Citizens of Halifax 1853

The Sailors of the H.M.S. Cumberland

Alexander Allen – The Victim
James Baldwin – Sees Allen's body
Peter Lawrie– Fights with Allen
William Giles – Allen's friend
Anthony Bambridge – Allen's friend
Richard Davis
Henry Freeman
Joseph McCathe

The Keeper and Employees of the Waterloo Tavern

Thomas Murphy – Waterloo Tavern-keeper, Witness, Accused of
    Allen's murder
John Gordon – Mysterious resident, Witness, Accused of Allen's
    murder
David Parsons – Handyman, Witness
Matilda Ballard – Prostitute, Witness
Sarah Myers – Prostitute, Witness
Jane O'Brien – Cook, Witness
Mary Anne Cole – Housekeeper, Prostitute
Thomas Shortis – Fiddler

The Police and City Officials

John Shehan – Watchman on duty
Maurice Power – Watchman on duty
James Clarke – City Clerk
Patrick Caulfield – Policeman on duty
James Wilson – Jailor

The Doctors

Dr. Jason Allan – Autopsy Doctor
Dr. John Slayter – Assistant at the autopsy
Dr. Thomas Fraser – Ship's Surgeon on the H.M.S. *Cumberland*

The Witnesses

Joseph Howe – Publisher, Politician
Samuel Young – Keeper of an Albemarle Street tavern where
　　　　　　Alexander Allen fights
William Newcomb – Clerk of the Market, Witness to Allen's fight
James O'Donnell – Witness to Allen's fight on Albemarle Street
John Patterson – Fisherman, Witness to events outside the Waterloo
　　　　　　Tavern
Richard Powell – Farmer, Witness to events outside the Waterloo
　　　　　　Tavern
Richard McCabe – Keeper of an Albemarle Street tavern where
　　　　　　Alexander Allen was seen

The Judge and the Attorneys

Thomas Chandler Haliburton – Trial Judge
William Young – Attorney General, Lawyer for the Government
W.Q. Sawyers – Attorney for the Accused
W.A. Johnston – Attorney for the Accused

Map of Downtown Halifax

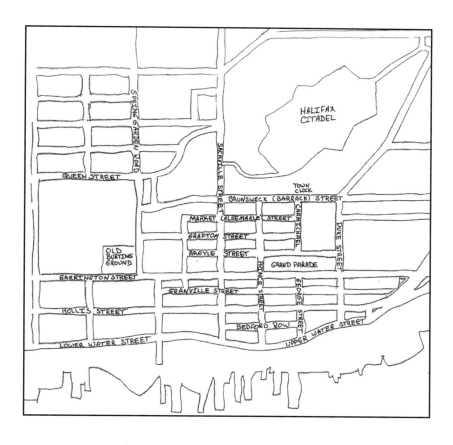

Chapter 1

The Graveyard

Not so long ago, on an unusually warm day in early autumn, I found myself lying face-up on a comfortable stretch of grass between two old, flaking tombstones in Halifax, Nova Scotia's, oldest graveyard, St. Paul's Cemetery. Established in 1749, the year of the city's founding, the cemetery is a national historic treasure, situated on an acre or so of green space in the city's downtown where, coincidentally, there also exists the largest concentration of pubs per capita in North America. This, also coincidentally, leads me back to where I began: lying face-up, on a comfortable stretch of grass, between two old, flaking tombstones, in the city's oldest graveyard.

I chose to lie there on that warm autumn day because it seemed to me – at the time, anyway – to be a fitting place to contemplate my Muse. And of all the things to muse upon while lying face-up in a graveyard between two old, flaking tombstones, I chose to muse upon this: what is it that lies beneath the lion's balls?

Let me explain.

At the entrance to the cemetery through which I'd walked, there stands an enormous stone archway with the words "Welsford" and "Parker" engraved in large letters, deep-set in thick stone. This huge, thirty-foot monument, built in 1857 as an ode to the British Empire, honoured the memory of two Nova Scotians – Major A.F. Welsford and Captain W.B.C.A. Parker – who fought and died in the Crimean War, which raged on the eastern edge of Europe between 1853 and 1856. Since I'd found myself lying some twenty feet from this monument, and since it was the largest object in my sight line – particularly given my horizontal position on the grass – I earnestly assessed its carved letters and myriad numbers.

After awhile, I found myself thinking about the nature and meaning of war memorials. And I found myself wondering what bit of enlightened British propaganda compelled nineteenth-century Nova Scotians who – as is generally true of all wars – were mostly poor, with little prospects, to pack up their belongings and travel for weeks, sometimes months, by boat, train, and foot to the dusty, eastern edge of Europe to fight a war on some forgettable stretch of sand and stone thrusting out between the Sea of Azov and the Black Sea.

I supposed that it was the Age of Empire, after all, with the French, the Germans, the Russians, the Turks, and the English among others, all vying for global preeminence. And, of course, this attractive stretch of sand and stone between the Sea of Azov and the Black Sea had been repeatedly invaded and occupied, by the Goths, the Huns, the Scythians, the Khazars, the Greeks, the Kipchaks, the Mongols, the Ottoman Turks, and now – to the great consternation of the French and the English – the Russians, who claimed to be the official protectors of Christianity in the largely Muslim Holy Land. Did these Nova Scotians go for Religion, Honour, Empire, or Romance? Lying there, I couldn't quite imagine how any Nova Scotian, or anyone one else for that matter, could be passionate or patriotic enough, religious or romantic enough to lay down his life for the British Empire in some ill-defined effort to help the French, Turks, and Sardinians steal the port of Sevastopol from the Russians.

The question of why these Nova Scotians did go seemed particularly pertinent to me, lying there, face-up between two old tombstones, because Nova Scotians were still, a good century and a half later, travelling by train and foot and now plane to other forgettable stretches of sand and stone on other far away lands to fight other wars for Religion, Honour, Romance, and Empire – this time Pax Americana.

Clearly, I was missing something.

Back then, the war for Empire had a most convincing Nova Scotian salesman – Old Joe Howe, the prominent Haligonian publisher of the *Novascotian* newspaper, the pugnacious politician who brought responsible government to Nova Scotia, and the vociferous advocate for Victorian values and Industrial Age progress. He was the ardent and articulate defender of Empire and of the Canadian colonies' responsibility to provide military support to the mother country in her international engagements. In fact, Howe even travelled to the United States, encouraging poor Irish Immigrants in America to enlist in the British cause. "There is no prison so loathsome in which I would not cheerfully have spent five years," Howe would say, "to have placed five regiments, in the spring of 1855, under the walls of Sebastopol."

That said, Howe's proselytizing for the British in the United States ignited the embers of ethnic division back in Halifax, where pro-British English Protestants clashed with anti-British Irish Catholics, immigrants who had been arriving in Halifax in great numbers since before the Irish famine, and who were, in these early years of the Victorian era, the largest and poorest ethnic group in Halifax. As things turned out, a prominent Irishman in Halifax informed the New York Press of Howe's efforts and, in doing so, dissuaded some sixty New York Irishmen from enlisting. The British soon found themselves in a diplomatic row with the Americans over Howe's efforts for Empire. Howe returned to Nova Scotia furious with Irish Haligonians. "Mercurial Irishmen will do well to remember," Howe gently threatened, "they are but a handful of the population ... Their best security is law and order, and the preservation of the free institutions of the country." Still, despite Irish resistance, Howe was convincing enough. Many Nova Scotians made their way to the Crimean War.

So I looked again, long and hard, at the Welsford-Parker Memorial and asked: was it possible that for all their troubles in the Crimea – for being shot through the head or the heart or the stomach, left to die, bleeding on some lonesome stretch of Black Sea sand and stone, singing "God Save the Queen" – that these Nova Scotians believed that their sacrifice would be honoured by their city and fellow citizens of the Empire with a nicely carved, brownstone arch?

Somehow, I doubted that.

After all, being dead, Major A.F. Welsford and Captain W.B.C.A. Parker would have hardly appreciated the thought. More likely, the Welsford-Parker monument was built for the other Haligonians, those living in the Age of Sail in this city by the sea, designed to elicit romantic passions for the dirty work of the Empire in faraway lands. If these notions were so, then they would nicely explain the other notable feature of this monument: the enormous stone lion standing atop the arch.

Looking at this fearsome beast, I gave some thought to the people, young and old, walking past each day. What did they think when they saw it? The question reminded me of a darkly funny tale – an apocryphal myth or foggy Halifax memory, I couldn't remember which – that I'd heard about this great stone lion.

A few years after the statue was built, and the lion was affixed at the top, a gaggle of tea-drinking Halifax matrons took embarrassed exception to that part of the lion that hung, well, liberally and prominently beneath the lion's tail. Concerned that this offending stone member's member might irreparably corrupt the morals of Halifax's passing youth, these prim spokeswomen of British gentility promptly demanded that the city fathers remove the hanging bits of the lion's well-endowed granite groin – presumably with a well-aimed chisel.

Imagine that.

I smiled at the juxtaposition of moral offenses: the stone lion's 'natural' appendage versus the celebration, in thick symmetrical stone, of war's great glory.

It was all so absurd.

But then again, maybe it wasn't. Halifax, after all, was built on the bones of just this kind of madness, of sailors and soldiers and citizens who died preparing to wage war in faraway lands. All around me, in fact, just a few feet beneath the earth, lay the bones of a thousand or more citizens whose reason for being in Halifax was, simply enough, to build and maintain military might for the protection and expansion of the Empire, the ghostly memory of which still echoed each day, at precisely noon, with the thudding boom of cannon fire from atop the fortress on Citadel Hill.

Lying there on the grass, staring up at this enormous memorial to the Crimean War dead, I wondered about this old city, wondered about its history, wondered about its people – the everyday people – who lived their lives here. All around me, carved in faded letters on cold stones, were the names of the city's first generations, names being slowly erased by time, wind, and rain; names shaped by the history that permeated the first hundred years of Halifax.

I recalled that, somewhere in an unmarked corner of this cemetery, likely over my left shoulder, there lay the earth-worn bones and dust of the city's first murder victim, Abraham Goodsides, a poor boatswain from the ship *Beaufort* – one of the original thirteen ships, filled with soldiers, sailors, and settlers that sailed into Chebucto harbour to found the city of Halifax. The young boatswain was stabbed to death somewhere along the rocky beach, not far from where I lay, just below the scattering of tents and felled trees that were the meagre sum of Halifax in late August of 1749.

Goodsides's killer, a Swiss sailor named Peter Carteel, may have been half-mad from the long sea voyage from England. Or he may have been unnerved by the constant threat of retaliation by the Mi'kmaq natives, whom the settlers had thoroughly harassed. Or perhaps he was weary from the labour of clearing trees and building fences and constructing houses. Then again, he may have been shaken by the explosive thunderstorms that swept through the tenuous settlement the day before, storms unlike anything he or any of the other settlers had heard or seen back home. Or perhaps Carteel found sorrow or rage at the bottom of a rum bottle and let the warm liquid play the devil with his disposition. Or maybe poor Abraham Goodsides just got in Peter Carteel's way. Whatever the reason, on a clear, cool Saturday evening in late August of 1749, Carteel felt compelled to punch a knife into Abraham Goodsides's chest and kill him. The stabbing had been the fifth since the settlers arrived just weeks earlier – but it was the first that resulted in murder.

For this crime, justice came swiftly.

Carteel was tried and convicted on the last day of August, 1749, and hanged by the neck two days later, on September 2, by the branch of an old hardwood tree – the city's first, and oft used, gallows – which stood on the same stretch of beach where Goodsides had been murdered.

No doubt, the irony was lost on Carteel.

Gently shifting my place on that comfortable stretch of grass, I thought of the general darkness that must have enveloped Halifax in the late eighteenth century, a time and place in this city almost beyond physical memory. In my travels to this and other old city graveyards, I looked with care at the early tombstones, gleaning some sense of the past. In this cemetery, for instance, I had seen headstones etched with haunting death-head skulls and bat-like wings, tombstones filled with gothic lettering, recording for posterity the lamentable tales of hard-lived, short lives. Reading these stones, I could almost feel the persistent chill of winter, the angry growl of hunger, and the terrifying fear of Mi'kmaq reprisal. Of course, these were just faint echoes of the city's past. Beyond these tombstones, and two or three old wooden buildings tucked away in dark corners of the city's core, this part of the past had no physical presence.

Only the ghosts remained.

Still, these ghosts remained prominent. The city's long past intertwined with modern-day tourism, fueling images – more imagined than real – of old Halifax: colourful town criers and swaggering privateers and resettled New England Loyalists who drew history-starved Yanks north each year, hunting for family history in the Nova Scotia Archives. Certainly, 1749 through 1814 lived large in the city's memory.

By contrast, the oldest existing physical bones of the city – the many late-Victorian buildings and homes built after 1860 – spoke of a prosperous early-modern era in Halifax. In other city graveyards, like Fort Massy Cemetery and Holy Cross Cemetery, I had seen in the post-1850 tombstones, gentle cherub heads with angelic wings above crisp, warm lettering, speaking of fuller lives filled with noteworthy accomplishments – for some, that is.

Before Queen Victoria's reign (1837-1901), most of Halifax's first generation – save for a scattering of aristocrats, bureaucrats, and a few pre-industrial age businessmen – shared a roughly equivalent social stature: the middling poor to the very poor. The Golden Age of Sail and The Age of Empire – converging with the Age of Victoria – created tremendous wealth for many. But it also created sharp economic and social divisions. Labourers, servants, merchants, shopkeepers, privateers, sailors, craftsmen, soldiers, and some aristocrats found themselves competing for the soul of Halifax in the context of historical forces at work beyond Halifax's city limits – a radical reorganization of work and society. Would Halifax embrace this "Victorian" ethos, its industrialization, its social reforms, and its capital acquisition? Or would Halifax choose instead those values associated with an older tradition, one more attuned to the seasons – of seed and sail? Not without some irony, it was a young Joe Howe who recognized the essence of this historic moment.

In 1838, Joseph Howe was sailing across the Atlantic with another young harbinger of the coming Industrial Age – Thomas Chandler Haliburton, the author of the Sam Slick tales first published in Howe's newspaper, the *Novascotian*. These tales had become enormously popular, not only in Canada but also in Europe. And so, Howe and Haliburton travelled together to England to enjoy this literary recognition.

Along the way, as their vessel sailed east across the open Atlantic, they happened upon another ship of unfamiliar design heading west. It was a sail-less steamer, in which Joe Howe immediately saw the future. "On she came in gallant style," said Howe, "with the speed of a hunter, while we were moving with the rapidity of an ox cart."

Howe's imagery was noteworthy: the individualist hunter, dangerously on the prowl, seeking out new food, new resources; and the oxcart, doddering along, slow, plowing familiar earth, rooted in an older, established agricultural age. "Never," Howe continued, "did we feel so forcibly the contrast between the steamer and the sailing vessel." Howe, of course, meant his comment to be a metaphor of speed. But more to the point, it was a prophetic metaphor of the age: craftsmanship versus mass production, wind versus coal. How apt that the name of the steamer was the *Sirius* – the brightest star in the sky. The future – at least for young Joe Howe and Thomas Chandler Haliburton – seemed bright. Then again – in a delightful paradox of name, metaphor, and prophecy – Sirius sat in the constellation Canis Major. That is, Sirius was also known as the Dog Star.

Halifax's great economic moment came and passed with this transitional period, during this Golden Age of Sail, a stretch of time, coincidentally enough, that passed more or less between 1843 and 1857, as the city celebrated its past and its future, its centennial, and its coming Industrial Age. For those who benefited from this new age, those like Joe Howe and Thomas Chandler Haliburton, this emerging future was the very definition of progress. But for the poor, this new age only increased the downward pressure on their lives. For them, two futures emerged for Halifax between 1843 and 1857, one leading to the familiar and one leading to the strange. It was a time of striking transformation, a time when, as Karl Marx wrote in 1848, "all that is solid melts into air."

So why did those Nova Scotians travel to the Crimea in 1854 to fight a war that was meaningless to their immediate lives? I still couldn't say. But I suspected the answer lay in a better understanding of the people and their times. It lay in a better understanding of what, exactly, melted in to air – and what, exactly, didn't. I thought once more about Major Welsford and Captain Parker.

On September 8, 1855, Major Welsford led an assault on the Great Redan, a portion of the Sevastopol fortification. At the head of his troops, Welsford raced across an open field, under constant fire, to the fortress walls. There, amid the chaos of cannon shot, smoke, and noise, he climbed a long wooden ladder laid against the stone. As Welsford reached the ladder's top, he thrust his head above the edge only to find that, at that same moment, a Russian cannon had been fired – and Major Welsford's head was blown off. In the same assault, Captain Parker also managed to make his way to the ladder. And he also managed to scale the wall. Unlike Welsford, he made his way inside the fortress. But by the time he did, the British were already in retreat. In the chaos that followed, Parker was riddled with bullets and died.

In October of 1855, a friend of Major Welsford sent the following letters to *The Times* of London:

> To the Editor of *The Times*
> Sir,
>
> You love to do justice to the brave and good. I therefore enclose to you a letter from one who was both in an eminent degree – the lamented Major Welsford of the 97th Regiment, written on the fatal morning of the 8th of September. Within the hour that he laid down his pen he was blown to atoms from the cannon's mouth, as described by your own inimitable correspondent. Few could have used it so at such a moment. Her Majesty has lost a devoted soldier, and I my dearest friend.
>
> > I am, Sir, your obedient servant,
> > Alfred Bennett

*

> My dear Bennett,
>
> This is about to be an eventful day to some of us, as we are to storm the Redan, the French the Malakoff; and as you say, 'would it were bedtime, Hal, and all were well.' But I trust in Providence all will be well, and that I shall be instrumental in making Her Majesty a present of the Redan, as I am to lead the Light Division storming party; and if God spare me, to be the first in and first up. This is to be done by escalade. I am glad Her Majesty has seen my photographs, and I now send you some more of them. No time for writing more, as the drums are going,
>
> Remember me to Lady ____. They asked me if I liked the idea of active service. I will tell them more about it when the day is over.
>
> God Bless you, my dear Bennett.
>
> > Believe me most truly yours,
> > A.F. Welsford

"Blown to atoms from the cannon's mouth" … "All that is solid melts into air …"

I rose to my feet, breathing in deeply the warm air, wondering if autumn weather would ever come. I looked around me, looked at the stone wall and at the iron fence that the builders of the Welsford-Parker Memorial wrapped around this graveyard. Nova Scotian author Thomas Raddall once said of this iron fence that the builders built it "to keep the ghosts where they belonged." I then headed for the gate, passing again through the arch of the Welsford-Parker Memorial. As I did, I playfully asked myself: so, what is it that lies beneath the lion's balls? Stepping out onto Barrington Street, and heading south into a steady breeze, I answered the question.

We do.

Walking along Barrington Street, I couldn't stop thinking about Nova Scotians and the Crimea, and about the lives lived in Halifax between 1840 and 1860. And though I didn't quite realize it at the time, I had in that moment begun a hunt for Halifax, for its past, for its ghosts, and for a "most mysterious affair."

A "most mysterious affair" born in a small pool of blood at the bottom of a tavern's front stairs.

Chapter 2

The Hill

I doubt Dante Alighieri – the medieval Italian poet who spent enormous amounts of time cooking up the excruciating details of hell – was much fun at a pub. Yet it's Dante I think of on a hot and humid August afternoon, as I open the thick wooden door to a corner tavern, a two-storey brick affair, just below the southeastern slope of Citadel Hill.

"All hope abandon ye who enter here," wrote Dante in his *Divine Comedy*. He was speaking literally of Hell, of course, and I was walking into the air-conditioned cool of a lively tavern on a hot summer's day. Still, his words seemed apt. I was entering this place in search of a dark mystery, one that, for the moment anyway, hid itself in the past, like an old schooner sailing into the familiar fog of Halifax Harbour.

The mystery?

I was on the trail of a cold-case murder – a murder case 150-years cold.

Clearly, I needed a beer.

So I make my way past two waist-high, rounded tables, each with two hip-high rounded stools, to another rounded table with accompa-

nying stools tucked into a corner by a small, two-pane window overlooking the street. I gently push aside the wooden condiments holder
and plastic-covered menu, place my ball cap and bag on the table,
and pull out a stool to sit. Almost immediately, a waitress appears at
my elbow.

About five and a half feet tall, with brown eyes and shoulder-
length hair, the waitress wears a brown skirt cut just above her ankles
over which she has tied a black apron with wide pockets. Above this,
she wears a white, low-cut, ruffled drawstring chemise under a dark
green vest dotted with dime-sized buttons. You could see where the
owners of this faux Victorian tavern were going with this. What would
an old style Victorian tavern be without a buxom serving wench? Her
clothes were designed to accentuate her bosom for lunch hour businessmen and university students hunting a midday beer buzz.

"How are you today?" she chirps, but doesn't wait for an answer.
She moves deftly to her real question: "Can I get you something to
drink?"

"I'll have," I say, but the thought trails off as I look to the
board above the bar. My waitress gives a tight, dutiful grin suggest-
ing strained patience while I decide what colour beer I want: brown,
red, or amber. I review the offerings and finally see what I like. "A
Rickard's Red," I say, "thanks." The waitress gives a faint nod and
walks off to the bar, no doubt glad to give her grin a rest.

Meantime, I look around.

In the early afternoon, the place is half filled with tourists hiding
from the heat and local twenty-somethings gearing up for a rowdy
night on the town. As much as things change in Halifax, they stay
the same. I turn to my right and look out the window, admiring the
grass of Citadel Hill sloping down to an iron fence sitting atop a
stone wall. Below the wall, along the sidewalk, tourists in t-shirts and
knee-length shorts stroll leisurely in both directions.

My attention returns to the room when the tavern door snaps
open and a dozen tourists tumble in. Loud and brash, they announce
themselves as a crowd of cruise ship patrons, in port for the day.
They chatter aimlessly at the door while surveying the tavern, until
they decide on three tables sitting close together, not far from me.

In some age-old tribal arrangement, the women gather together in a tight group around one table, while the men gather more loosely, standing and leaning, around the other two. They talk loudly with nasal accents and missing "Rs."

One round-faced man with a marine crewcut and narrow eyes takes charge. He thumps his right fist on the table for comic effect and yells to the barkeep, "We need beer here!" A woman sitting next to him coughs a rough, raspy laugh that speaks of too many cigarettes and not enough exercise.

Answering the man's call – or perhaps his challenge – another tavern wench approaches, offering a familiar, dutiful grin. At their table, she cuts the obligatory greeting, already knowing where this is going, and gets to the point. "What would you like to drink?" she asks.

"Well," says one patron, "what've ya got?"

The waitress mechanically recites the beer list, foreign and domestic. After a game of twenty questions ("Is that light or dark?" "Where's that from?") they decide on a local brew. She nods and turns away from the table, making her way across the tavern to the bar and orders Keith's beer for everyone. Amused by the sideshow, I smile to myself. But with that pressing drink decision made, I look back out the window to the street that runs north to south beneath Citadel Hill.

It has been called many names. For the last hundred years, it has been called Brunswick Street, a pleasant, almost genteel, aristocratic reference to Georgian England. But this genteel name, Brunswick, is darkly and ironically funny. "What's in a name?" Shakespeare once asked of a rose. When it comes to this street, the answer is "much."

On another hot August day, more than 250 years earlier, in 1749, Edward Cornwallis, travelling from England, sails into Chebucto Harbour to settle the town of Halifax. He is confronted by land grown thick and dark with trees from the rocky waterfront to the rolling hills beyond. With no obvious place to come ashore and settle a town, Cornwallis asks his official surveyor, Captain Charles Morris, to find a desirable site and to design a suitable town plan.

With a good memory about poor choices made in settling Louisbourg – that windswept French fortress in Cape Breton that forever found itself bracing against the relentless winds and storms of the North Atlantic – Captain Morris eyes the eastern slope of a hill, a mile or two in from the harbour's mouth, just past a small island that would be named for King George. The site is well away from the rough Atlantic wind and well placed on a desirably defensible peninsula. So Captain Morris proposes the site to Cornwallis, and Cornwallis and his officers quickly agree: this will be the place.

Soon thereafter, while Captain Morris sets to work designing his town, a motley group of soldiers, sailors, and settlers – an unprepared rabble lured to this wild shore with promises of free land and free food for a year – begin the arduous work of felling trees and clearing brush under the constant threat of conflict with the aggrieved Mi'kmaq natives, to whom the English have been anything but cordial. Since most settlers are not familiar with the skills and effort necessary for clearing land, the work is slow, poorly organized and badly executed.

Still, some weeks later, on September 14, 1749, Morris finally presents his plan for the new town to Cornwallis and his officers. The town is to be called Halifax – in honour of George Montague Dunk, Master of the Buckhounds, President of the Board of Trade, the Earl of Halifax, and the sponsor of this settlement. The town of Halifax is to have a dozen streets, laid out on a logical, Enlightenment-era grid, six by six, with blocks precisely 320 feet by 120 feet. Each street, by design, will be precisely sixty feet wide and each block will have precisely sixteen lots, forty feet wide by sixty feet deep. At its centre, a splendid gathering space will be created called the Grand Parade. The execution of the plan, however, is somewhat less than precise. The first maps of the city reveal thirty-five blocks with fourteen nameless streets, all more or less fifty-five feet wide.

The first settlers of Halifax are given their free land in these thirty-five city blocks by drawing lots, and once won, the lots are quickly developed. The first homes are rough wooden huts and canvas tents. Equally ramshackle, the town's first protection is a winding fence made of upright logs with carved points that run from the waterfront, up the hill, around the town, and down again to the water's edge. Attached to this fence, roughly equidistant from each other, are five rudimentary, squared wooden blockhouses, providing bored sentries basic protection from the cold, the rain, and the occasional bullet.

As for the first streets, they are mud and stump-filled lanes that will be, for years, nearly impassable in bad, and sometimes even in good, weather. Later, new generations, feeling the first hints of civic pride, began naming the streets, honouring notable persons here and abroad. George Street, for instance, is named for the reigning king, George II; Prince Street named, logically enough, for the prince; Granville Street is named for the Right Honourable George Granville, a prominent statesmen of the time; Barrington Street named for the Viscount Barrington of Ardglass; Grafton Street named for the Duke of Grafton; Albemarle (later Market) Street named for the Duke of Albemarle; Blowers Street for Sampson Salter Blowers, Chief Justice of Nova Scotia; Argyle Street for Archibald Campbell, the Duke of Argyle; and so on.

But the top street of this young town, the street highest on the hill, the street just below the western defenses, running from Sackville Street in the south (where the south barracks are located) to Buckingham Street in the north (where the north barracks are located) is given the decidedly utilitarian, almost afterthought name – Barrack Street. It is, after all, just a street for common soldiers.

As with similar streets in similar ports around the world, Barrack Street quickly acquires grog houses, brothels, and broken down tenements. The sailors, soldiers, and working-class locals who nightly walk this street soon call it The Hill. Still others, those with some wit and mindful of the boisterous arguments and bloodletting brawls that often occur on Barrack Street, called it "Knock 'em Down Street." Though all the streets of Halifax in those early years can be described as dangerous, Barrack Street stands out as the most dangerous of all – a place where the rougher sort regularly congregate to forget their troubles with rum, dance, and prostitution. Locals say that "for people to go to [that] district after 'candle lighting time' could be considered a bid for trouble."

Back in my modern theme park tavern, I am imagining what

troubles the rougher sort might find in those early days on Barrack Street, when my waitress returns carrying my single pint of Rickard's Red on a large circular tray. Deftly, she reaches across the table, snaps down a small cardboard coaster, and on it places my tapered glass of beer.

"Thanks," I offer.

She looks up with her dutiful grin and nods. "You're welcome," she says then heads off to another table in the centre of the tavern, where two beefy young men in t-shirts, shorts, and ball caps stare for an unrepentant moment at her exposed bosom. She gives them a strained-patience grin and asks what they'd like to drink. They grin back, thinking they're charming her.

Unlikely, I suspect.

While the boys continue their charm offensive, two other waitresses cross the tavern floor with trays of Keith's beer. They deliver froth-topped glasses to the cruise ship crowd, who, on seeing the beer, murmur their collective approval. When the glasses land on the table, the crowd makes short work of the light-yellow brew, and even before the waitresses make their way back to the bar, the group is roaring for another round. The big guy with the crewcut, thinking it may help move the order along, launches into a rousing, off-tune chorus of "When Irish Eyes Are Smiling."

His mates just laugh.

Meantime, I sip at my pint of Rickard's Red, and with my elbow on the table and my hand on my chin, I look again out the window at Barrack Street, imagining the city some 250 years earlier, imagining one event I read about in an early newspaper.

On a cloudless Monday night, in early April of 1754, a lonely soldier staggers through the streets of Halifax after a long night of drinking and dancing in the grog shops along The Hill. Slowly and deliberately, he tries to avoid the mud, ruts, and puddles. But despite his efforts, the rum gets the better of him. He stumbles heavily against a house and runs his elbow through a quarrel of glass. Then, lurching off the wall, he falls into the street.

The sound of glass breaking wakes the single resident of the house, a man. Startled, he jumps to his feet, sees the window and the glass on the floor, and heads for the door, grabbing his cutlass along the way. Outside, the man finds the drunken soldier lying in the street in front of his house. The soldier, stunned by the fall and thick-headed from the rum, sees the house owner holding his cutlass, so he pushes himself to his feet to take up the challenge.

Immediately, the man with the cutlass responds. He steps forward and makes two swift motions. He thrusts the cutlass into the soldier's body, pulls it out, and thrusts it in again. The soldier, stunned by the suddenness of the actions, looks to his stomach, clutches his wounds, and falls to his knees. With blood appearing in his hands, the soldier rolls to the ground and looks up. The man with the cutlass, eyes wild with rage, swings his cutlass downward at the soldier one final time and cuts "off three of his toes thro' a new pair of double channel pumps, sole and all."

How the fight ended and whether or not the soldier died are facts lost to the past. However, given the rough justice of the time, the man with the cutlass was certainly imprisoned. And had the solider died – a strong likelihood given his horrible wounds – the man with the cutlass would have been hanged at the waterfront gallows, on the branch of that sturdy hardwood tree.

I am drawn away from my thoughts of the past yet again when one of the cruise ship crowd, a big-haired woman in a white t-shirt and blue jeans, pulls out a digital camera and starts snapping pictures. Delighted, a half dozen members of the group pull out their digital cameras and start snapping pictures, leaving the tavern momentarily flashing like a disco. But the flashes stop when the group hears the opening guitar lick on the house stereo. It's the Animals, "The House of the Rising Sun." The novice photographers toss their cameras to the tables and collectively sing the opening lines: "There is a house in New Orleans, they call the rising sun, and it's been the ruin of many a poor boy and God, I know I'm one." When the chorus is finished, the group members spontaneously cheer and then convulse into peals of laughter.

I take another drink of my Rickard's Red, and think again about the man with the cutlass hanging at the end of a swaying rope. I think, too, of the first hundred years of Halifax's history. Even as the city emerged economically and socially as a major port, the dark character of Barrack Street changed little, except to firmly establish its mean reputation as the last vestige of an old garrison town. When the Victorian Age arrived in 1837, and the Golden Age of Sail emerged with it, the numbers of soldiers and sailors making their way to Halifax and to The Hill only increased. And with them came the troubles.

In real a sense, after 1837, two different cities emerged on the shores of Chebucto – one for the upwardly mobile middle class who gratefully adapted to the changing values and expectations of the Victorian Age, and one for the entrenched, forgotten poor, those left out of the emerging prosperity and who, as a consequence, relied on the values and expectations of the past for comfort in difficult times.

Unavoidably, this created class tensions.

The wealthier population of Halifax wanted the blight of The Hill contained. So the police – Halifax's new Victorian agents of social order, established in 1846 – were engaged to do just this: contain, but not stop, the drunkenness, the prostitution, the brawls, and the crimes of Knock 'em Down Street (which, by now, had expanded to the street below it, Albemarle – today called Market Street).

Why just contained?

As a port town, Halifax was different than other towns its size. The social classes engaged in a peculiar symbiotic dance, one that gave an unspoken tolerance for darker habits. These habits, fed with money from a transient population of soldiers and sailors, contributed greatly to the city's wealth. The two worlds of Halifax – the rich and the poor – lived separate lives with separate values and separate expectations, and yet they lived, literally, side-by-side. It was a unique balancing act. Mind, this balance could be tipped. Even among the citizens of Barrack Street, the dark habits could be intolerable.

Drinking my pint, I imagine another hot August night on Barrack Street in 1838, when, not far from where I sit, nearly 3,000 citizens gathered on the eastern slope of Citadel Hill under a clear, moonlit sky, to cheer the violent destruction of one notorious tavern.

In the humidity of a summer night, a sailor is "horribly beaten" and then murdered in a tavern along Barrack Street. Word spreads, and by the next evening, a group of angry Barrack Street citizens decide that they will end the steady stream of problems emanating from the notorious pub, problems that cross even the murky social code of Barrack Street.

That evening, with the sun having set behind Citadel Hill and the Old Town Clock, citizens crowd together on the eastern slope of the hill and cheer the assembled rioters who enter the tavern. Inside, the rioters tear out the widow frames, toss the beds and bedding into the street, break up the tables and benches of the taproom, and smash the liquor bottles – but not before they quench their considerable thirst, of course.

Outnumbered by the crowd that night, the policemen only watch, waiting for the rioters to grow weary. When they do, the law establishes order, making arrests and dispersing the crowd. Later, when the arrested rioters are brought before the courts, most are acquitted – a tacit approval of street justice that speaks to the peculiar balance of Halifax's social structure.

Back in my modern-day tavern, I hear music in strange counterpoint to the in-house stereo. The big-haired woman who started the digital camera frenzy has now produced a small, portable music player from her purse and has turned up the volume. From the tinny speakers, I hear a vaguely familiar calypso tune and watch some of the cruise ship crowd playfully dance. While the happy crew enjoys its dance and its second round, I think more about this city in transition, about the space of time between the closing of the old cemetery and the building of the Welsford-Parker Memorial. I think, too, about the emerging sets of values – of the rising middle class and the falling transient class – that existed in symbiotic counterpoint. And I think about the revealing moments when the two worlds occasionally met.

In late July of 1842, a relatively prosperous young American writer named Richard Henry Dana, Jr., author of *Two Years Before the Mast*, ventures out of his comfortable social circle and makes his way along Barrack Street recording his impressions. That night, out on The Hill,

Dana sees two prostitutes "accosting men for bad purposes." "One of the girls [is] young," he writes, "with an interesting face." Perhaps she is new to the base rhythm of enticing men to a bed or a dark alley, because she seems to Dana to be shy and uncertain. The other girl, however, is all too practiced at her craft. Dana notes how she "boldly" approaches another man. When that man turns her down, Dana finds himself the object of her attention. She eyes the young American and steps close to proposition him. The embarrassed writer declines. He then looks again into the eyes of the younger girl, who drops her gaze to the ground. He considers her for a moment, wondering about her plight, wondering how he might make a difference in her life. But his attention is diverted when he hears shouts at the south end of Barrack Street.

He looks over his shoulder and sees a young soldier being chased by a "bloodthirsty crowd," yelling as they run, "down with him, kill him, knock him over." One man, running at the lead of the crowd, manages to reach the soldier and strikes him in the head. The soldier falls to the ground. Two or three men also reach the soldier and strike more blows. When money falls from the soldier's pocket, the crowd's attention is momentarily diverted. In the confusion, the terrified soldier staggers to his feet and starts running again, tripping frantically toward the barracks' gates. When the crowd realizes the soldier is moving, they take up the chase.

Cries from sentries at the barrack's gates arouse a dozen soldiers "dressed in their long grey coats & high cloth caps." They rush to the gates with muskets and bayonets at the ready. There, they find the desperate soldier, collapsed. From the ground the soldier identifies the troublemakers. The guards immediately press into the crowd and return "with three or four prisoners, rowdyish looking fellows, whom they [place] in the watch house." When the crowd finally disperses from the barrack gates, Dana realizes with some disappointment that the prostitutes are gone. So he returns to his walk along The Hill, watching and writing.

The taverns, brothels, and tenement houses, he notes, vary in shape and size, but they share a common trait: "filth" and "decay." He notes that the taverns are crowded. In the grog shops along the street, he sees soldiers, sailors, labourers, prostitutes, and drifters moving constantly in and out. To Dana, it seems the street gathers together a chaotic mass of Halifax's poorest people with the transient men of the Citadel and the sea. The taverns hum relentlessly with sound and activity. Twenty, thirty, or more men and a dozen or more women crowd themselves happily into a single room. In one tavern, Dana sees a fiddler playing. The fiddler sits on one of two wooden chairs, stomping his foot heavily, keeping time on the wooden plat-form while the patrons dance. In the other chair, another musician plays a tambourine. When the patrons are not dancing, they sit and talk at the rough built benches and tables, or lean, relaxed, against the blackened walls.

From the tavern-keeper at the opposite end of the room, the patrons buy their drinks, anything from the light, locally made ginger beer to the heavy rum of the West Indies. The tavern-keeper, Dana notes, is "bloated" and "red faced," watching the goings-on with a careful eye, watching the girls taking men upstairs to their rooms, counting in his head his share of the money made.

Dana observes that the tavern's prostitutes look worn, like their tattered clothes. At a distance, one young woman appears "thin" with "good-features," "bright cheeks" and "black hair curling in ringlets from the top of her head." Up close, however, she smells strongly of brandy, and looks tired and shaken, her "skin tight to her bones," her "chest fallen in," her "eyes wild and sparkling from liquor, but with dark lines and cavities under them." Dana sees that she is trying to cover her weary look with bright ribbons tied in her hair. But too much is asked of the ribbons, and the effort fails. Instead, she looks little better than "a galvanized corpse." Another girl in the tavern is "thick-set," with "coarse" features. She is "pug nosed and pock marked." In fact, all the women, writes Dana, seem infected with dis-ease and decay.

Back in my tavern, I watch the cruise ship crowd. They have ordered a third round, gearing up for what promises to be a lively night on the town. I lift my glass in silent toast and drain the remain-der of my Rickard's Red. I then look across the room and see my waitress standing at another table. When she turns her head, I catch her eye and hold up my empty glass.

She nods.

I turn back to the window at my right, and I think about Dana, both an observer and a participant, and I am reminded why I entered this particular tavern in the first place. I came to get a tangible feel for this space; came to hunt for some hint of the past; came to sit, if possible, within a few feet – and 150 years' time – of a dead man.

Out on the street, the tourists still stroll along the sidewalk. I think of the strange juxtaposition of images in time – two taverns and two sets of tavern patrons, past and present. I consider the modern day "sailors" singing now a few tables away from me, all comfortably engrossed in the fatty riches of early twenty-first-century life, comfortably lit on a light-beer buzz in the very "space" where the "ruder sort" of Halifax lived on the rough, unforgiving edge of Victorian Age society.

My waitress arrives with my second pint. She forgets the dutiful smile – it's all business now. In two efficient motions, she picks up the empty glass and puts down the full one. Then she walks away, leaving me to my thoughts, my beer, and my cruise ship friends. I take another drink and remember again the words of Dante Alighieri: "All hope abandon ye who enter here." I find a pen and my notebook in my bag, put them on the table, and then methodically look around the tavern. From old newspapers and historical accounts, I've pieced together the physical details of a pub that once stood here – more or less where I sit. It was called the Waterloo Tavern.

I imagine it.

The Waterloo Tavern stands two houses in from the southwest corner of Barrack and Prince Streets facing west onto Citadel Hill. It is a three-storey affair, built with adze-hewn beams, mortised and framed with wooden pegs and split width lathes. It has a steeply pitched roof over the third floor with two dormer windows. Below them, three windows on the second floor face out onto the street. And below them, at the street level, a single window sits sandwiched between the two short staircases that lead to two narrow doors. The face of the building is covered with grey, weather-beaten shingles.

Up the north stairs from the street, a door leads into the tap-room, a large rectangular space with a bar at one end; tables, a few chairs, and benches in the middle; and a small platform with enough room for a fiddler and some dancers at the other. A moveable partition shuts the bar out from the taproom after hours. Hiding behind the bar, through a narrow doorway, is tucked the tavern-keeper's bedroom.

The south side door from the street opens into a modest vestibule. From here, on the left, another door leads to the taproom. Straight ahead, a narrow stairwell opens to the rooms above. These rooms are modest in size and furnishings, all for rent to sailors, transients, and prostitutes. Compared with other houses and taverns on Barrack Street, the Waterloo Tavern is wholly unremarkable – better than some, worse than others.

For a long while, I imagine this Waterloo Tavern, giving particular attention to the north side stairs that lead into the taproom, because it is here – roughly where I sit, drinking my second pint of Rickard's Red – in the first hours of September 8, 1853, that the body of a sailor lies inert in the shadows.

Something – or someone – had fractured his skull.

Chapter 3

The Body

According to the philosophy of abstractionism, the human mind acquires most or all of its concepts by abstracting them from personal experience, which means, in theory, that someone can abstract the general idea of, say, a "city" from a specific, experiential concept of, say, "Halifax." Then again, the eighteenth-century critics of abstractionism thought personal experience too vague to have any real meaning to be useful when thinking abstractly. In either case, it occurs to me that both the creators and critics of abstractionism clearly had too much time on their hands and that such considerations were mostly meaningless after drinking two pints of Rickard's Red.

Besides, I had a body to find – well, an abstract body, anyway.

So I pay my bill, leaving a generous tip for my serving wench, and head for the door. As I do, the cruise ship crowd is singing: "Hit the road, Jack, and don't ya come back no more, no more, no more, no more ..."

Maybe it's a good thing Ray Charles is no longer with us. This would have killed him.

I consider that I need to find a place where I can better visualize the death scene – the body lying against a staircase that no longer exists, by a tavern that no longer exists, on a street whose name no longer exists.

No problem.

Outside the tavern, I turn left on the sidewalk and cross at Prince Street. From there, I walk to Sackville Street, turn right, and cross in front of a blue and black Subaru with a Pennsylvania license plate. The driver, a tourist, is irritated by my uniquely Haligonian assumption that, in a crosswalk, the pedestrian has the right of way. Exasperated by my refusal to move quickly enough, he leans on his horn. Unmoved by his protest, I resist the urge to give the Pennsylvanian tourist my raised middle finger, choosing instead to offer my dutiful serving-wench grin. Not surprisingly, the Pennsylvanian tourist is hardly charmed. No matter. I manage to reach the sidewalk, and the disgruntled tourist moves on.

I continue walking west, up a steep slope of sidewalk pavement across from Artillery Park, which is still an active military site dating back some 200 years. Surrounded by a wrought iron fence, the park holds a collection of two-storey buildings – some wooden, some brick, all more than 100 years old – all situated on a well-groomed stretch of a dozen or so acres. At some point in time, the landscape designers, for reasons that aesthetically elude me, parked a half-dozen or more cannons – some with wooden wheels and others with rubber tires – willy-nilly about the grounds. Unable to explain their presence, I assume they are meant to keep confused tourists at bay – or at least bemused.

A dozen yards further along, I turn right onto a road that winds its way up the eastern face of Citadel Hill. Twenty yards beyond that I make one final right turn and step off the pavement, out onto the grass, and scan the ground for a suitable spot with a good view of Brunswick Street's south end. When I find a stretch of grass that will do, I sit and unzip my shoulder bag, removing a ballpoint pen, a six-by-ten black Hilroy notebook, and an old city map of Halifax. I then look across the street at the late-Victorian, two-storey brick tavern where I enjoyed my two pints of Rickard's Red and survey the block. The red brick tavern is attached on its north side to an unimaginative concrete slab of a building that runs half the block – a self-proclaimed cabaret. At the north side of the cabaret is also attached another modernist structure, a similarly slab-like concrete office building eight stories high with various tiers and decks, vaguely reminding me of the Hanging Gardens of Babylon.

Certainly, none of it reminds me of old Halifax.

That said, from the description I've read of the Waterloo Tavern, and roughly measuring out the original lot sizes in my mind, I know that the north stairs of the Waterloo sat close to where I had been sitting with my pints in the brick tavern. Once oriented to the site, I open my Hilroy notebook and remove about a dozen photocopied newspaper pages. I open one. At the top, the banner reads *The Daily Sun*, April 27, 1854. This issue was published the day following a trial for the murder of a sailor on Barrack Street, which occurred some seven months earlier. With the sun behind me, I hold the paper firmly in my hands and rest my elbows on my knees. I take a deep breath and begin reading the news of the day.

Then as now, the weather is a constant source of complaint. *The Daily Sun* reports that Halifax is in the grips of "unseasonably cold weather," with the streets "still covered in snow," and ice still covering parts of the Northwest Arm. In the column next to the weather report, I find another constant source of complaint, a biting editorial decrying the violence, vice, and drunkenness on the streets of Halifax. "The riots in our streets," it reads, "both day and night; the number of drunken persons, youths and others, constantly to be met with; the amount of gambling and dissipation; the desecration of the Sabbath; and the constant addition to the number of places of resort for all kinds of vice and immorality in our town are matters creating considerable uneasiness among the well-disposed and right-thinking part of our fellow townsmen."

I am struck again by the mirror similarity of Halifax, then and now.

I turn the page and read that trouble is brewing in the Crimea. The Russians, according to the report, are expanding their sphere of influence there. In response, the British and French have mobilized their own militaries. According to this report offered from the ship *Arabia* – presently anchored in the harbour – the first divisions of the

French have, in fact, arrived in Constantinople. Meantime, the Turks, allies of the British and the French, have already attacked the Russians with 12,000 troops near the town of Skripetz. The battle lasted four hours, ending with the Russians retreating, "leaving 600 dead on the field." All this is welcome news to readers in Halifax since its young men are fighting there.

Again, I turn the page and search the columns for news.

I see the headline for another story, and I wonder if the Haligonians reading it – 150 years ago – saw the connection between the Crimean crisis and the other news of the day: the riveting details of Thomas Murphy's trial, a trial for the murder, seven months earlier, in September 1853, of a sailor named Alexander Allen. Allen had been a sailor on the H.M.S. *Cumberland*, which left Halifax days after the murder to join the British Fleet near the Crimea. As well, the juxtaposition of this story against the editorial about violence and vice in the city makes me wonder if the anger among Halifax's citizens about civil decay and endemic violence is fuelled by the details of the Murphy trial, by the dark details of life and death on Barrack Street. I turn the page again and begin reading about the "supposed murder" of Alexander Allen.

By all accounts, September 7, 1853, was a dismal day.

I imagine a thick, grey fog creeping slowly off the water, rolling, unstoppable, onto the wharfs and warehouses along the waterfront; imagine it moving unhurriedly through George and Prince Streets, Sackville and Duke Streets. It drifts across the Cheapside Market at Bedford Row, rich with country-grown foods and imported manufactured goods, and slides in among the people, young and old as they hurry to and from their homes and businesses. It floats through the Grand Parade, at the city's centre, where the soldiers sometimes march, and the citizens sometimes complain. It reaches up, across the green, copper steeple of St. Paul's Church, the oldest building in the city, which has seen, for more than four generations now, every fog that has swallowed this city. It pushes on, over the most populous streets, over Grafton Street and Albemarle Street and Barrack Street. It surmounts Citadel Hill and Fort George, until finally, it rolls down the western slope of the hill and off into the trees beyond.

But I then imagine the fog blowing off, leaving behind a tired gloom and an overcast sky. The air is warm. September in Halifax always brings the summer's last breath, one final exhalation of heat over the city, a warmth that lulls its citizens into a false seasonal confidence before evaporating into the first chill blast of winter. Just the week before, in fact, on September 4, 1853, the temperature reaches a blistering eighty-six degrees, the hottest September day anyone then alive can remember.

I imagine the citizens of Halifax on that Wednesday in early September going about their business, buying and selling their wares along the streets and the waterfront, the noise of horses' hooves and wagons' wheels mixing with the constant clatter and chatter of merchants and shoppers, seamen and sailors. Prosperous times have come to Halifax in this Golden Age of Sail. More than ever, it seems, people have more money to spend. Each day, the newspapers announce a cornucopia of consumer goods, the newest wares and foods from home and abroad: glassware and china, coffee and tea, sugar and molasses, pork and beef, wine and spirits, cloth and clothes, cordage and leather – the choices seem endless.

The harbour, too, speaks expansively of the city's prosperity. It fills daily along the waterfront with ships whose masts, when seen from Citadel Hill, appear like a forest of limbless trees growing along the harbour's edge. Man-o-war ships, privateers, and merchant vessels tied up at the wharves. And when wharves fill, the ships anchor in the harbour, disgorging into rowboats their sailors and soldiers heading for adventure in the old garrison town.

Thirty years earlier, a British officer named William Moorson described the harbour and waterfront this way: "The wharves are crowded with vessels. Signals are constantly flying at the Citadel for vessels coming in; merchants are running about, in anticipation of their freight; officers of the garrison are seen striding down with a determined pace to welcome a detachment from the depot, or a pipe of Sneyd's claret for the mess; and ladies, tripping along a tip toe of expectation, flock into two or three soi-disant bazaars for the latest a-la-mode bonnets."

Still sitting on the hill, I pull from my black bag a small photo-copied painting by Robert D. Wilkie. Entitled "View of Halifax, Nova Scotia from the Red Mill Dartmouth," the painting shows a pastoral setting, woods and fields on the Dartmouth shore in 1853. The harbour fills the picture's background, and beyond it sprawls the bustling city of Halifax. On the Dartmouth side, in the foreground to the left, stands a large windmill. When the picture was painted, the windmill was still in operation with a waterwheel driving the gristmill inside. Notably, the windmill sits amid trees and an open field, while nearby are parked two horse-drawn carriages with large, wooden wheels.

When the viewer looks with care, a striking contrast emerges. The image of the still operating windmill stands in juxtaposition to the modern, nineteenth-century happenings in the harbour and in Halifax. The harbour is thick with sailing vessels, and below Fort George, on Citadel Hill, three or four stacks spew smoke – the first intimations, perhaps, of an emerging industrial age.

It is a snapshot of Halifax at a transitional moment in history.

I put down the picture and look again along Brunswick Street and think of that warm Wednesday in September. At dusk, the street lamps are lit, but their light is swallowed by the evening's gloom. Oddly, along Barrack Street, just below Citadel Hill, the gloom some-how seems welcome. On The Hill, from Sackville Street in the south to Buckingham Street in the north, sailors and soldiers, labourers and drifters walk along slowly, looking to spend what little money they have in their pockets on rum and dance and prostitution. They sing cheerfully, shout riotously, and swear angrily, filling the air with rowdy promise. Early as it is, the faint sound of a fiddle, maybe two, can be heard drifting out from the taverns. Already, women in worn dresses stand at the wooden doorways and alleyway entrances barking unashamedly bawdy enticements.

When daylight finally fades, the buzz of socializing along Bar-rack Street becomes a steady grumble. In the shadow of one tavern wall, a drunken sailor urinates. A passing soldier, disinclined to sail-ors by profession, steps forward and shoves the sailor's head against the shingles. The sailor, stunned, falls to his knees. He rolls onto his backside and curses his attacker. The soldier offers nothing but a cruel laugh. The enraged sailor then scrambles to his feet and charges. Both sailor and soldier fall into the street, swinging, clutching, and tearing. Passing patrons along Barrack Street simply ignore them.

The hours pass.

By eleven o'clock, the wave of drinking and dancing crests. The Barrack Street taverns have absorbed the thirsty bodies for hours and now begin disgorging rum-filled patrons – some walking, some staggering, some crawling – out into the shadows, heading down the street toward their rooms and their homes.

Most do, anyway.

Over the top of my newspaper, I look across Brunswick Street and imagine the Waterloo Tavern. I imagine the doorway that leads into the taproom. So too, I imagine the doorway that leads into a hallway vestibule and then up a stairwell to the second and third floors. There, in a rented room on the second floor, a carpenter and petty thief named John Gordon lies on a small bed half awake. He drifts lazily toward sleep, until he is startled by the sound of a sash falling from a window and then the breaking of glass. A moment later, he hears a thud against the front of the house, outside. He drops his feet to the floor, pulls on his pants and shirt, and then heads down the stairs to the taproom where he finds two more residents of the tavern, Sarah Myers, a tavern prostitute, and David Parsons, a workman about the house, sitting together at a corner table.

They look up when Gordon enters the room.

"My God," says Gordon as he runs to the door exiting to the street, "I think someone jumped from the window!"

On hearing Gordon's words, David Parsons also starts for the door. And so too, the tavern-keeper, Thomas Murphy, emerges from his room behind the bar and follows Parsons and Gordon to the door and out onto the step. There, in the shadows of the street, they see a form at the bottom of the stairs. Murphy pushes past Gordon and Parsons and steps down into the street. He turns and faces the body, then kneels to look closely. Carefully, he reaches out, takes the body by the shoulders and moves it into a sitting position. The shadows make seeing difficult, so Murphy turns the body further to the left, catching the faint light coming from the doorway. His stomach goes watery. The face – a man's face – is gashed and wet with blood. Worse still, Murphy knows him – a sailor who rented a room upstairs for the night.

His name is Alexander Allen.

Murphy looks up at Parsons and Gordon. "I believe the man is dead," he says. "What should we do?"

Stunned, Parsons and Gordon are unable to speak. They just stare at the body of Alexander Allen. Finally, Parsons shakes his head. "I don't know," he says. "I don't know."

Murphy releases the shoulders of Alexander Allen and the body rolls slowly forward, then to the side, and stops when the head rests against the lower stair. Murphy stands and looks at Parsons and Gordon. "Stay right here," he says, "I'll go for the watchman." They agree. Murphy runs north along Barrack Street, leaving Parsons and Gordon in the shadows, still staring at the bloodied body. After a time, Murphy will return with two men, watchmen named John Shehan and Maurice Power.

At least, this is the story as Murphy, Gordon, and Parsons tell it.

Looking from the hill to the site of the Waterloo, I find it odd that neither Parsons nor Myers claim to have heard the sound of breaking glass, and find it odder still that neither Parsons nor Myers heard the sound of a body falling against a house. Then again, Gordon's window may have been opened, and the taproom windows may have not. Such details have been lost to time. Still, the incongruity nags at me. That said, about what happens next, all agree – well, almost all.

Shehan, the old Irish watchman, recalls it this way: "My name is Shehan, and I am watchman on Barrack Street. I work the beat with my colleague, Maurice Power. On the night of September 7th, I passed the Waterloo Tavern about a quarter before twelve o'clock. The Waterloo Tavern is two houses in from the south corner of the block but one next to the corner of the street leaving past Artillery Park, where a sentry stands. All was quiet that night."

Although no record exists saying as much, I imagine Shehan

being large, even physically imposing. The clipped cadence of his words suggests a straightforward man, more used to breaking up fights on Barrack Street with a sharp word or force of personality than pondering an assailant's psychological motivations. I am struck by the matter-of-fact quality of his remembrances.

"We were going southward at the time," Shehan recalls, "and turned down by Mr. Rhind's Corner, and then turned to Albemarle Street. I was in Grafton, Albemarle, and Buckingham Corner that night. It was at the corner of Grafton and Buckingham Street that Thomas Murphy, the keeper of the Waterloo Tavern, came to me, and asked me to come down. It might have been half an hour after I passed the Waterloo Tavern. Murphy said that a serious accident had happened at his house, that a man had jumped out of the window and that he would not wish it on any account."

To get a sense of the distance travelled by Shehan, Power, and Murphy, I fold my newspaper into quarters and tuck it firmly into my notebook then slip the notebook into my bag. With my ball cap pulled low on my head and my bag pulled high over my shoulder, I stand and start walking north, along the grass, parallel to Brunswick Street, following the path that Murphy must have taken. I walk up behind the Old Town Clock and then down again toward Brunswick Street. Cars pass quickly, heading north, out of town. Ahead, beyond the grass of the hill, I see a gathering of high-rise buildings where Buckingham and Jacob Streets once ran from the waterfront to the west. Both streets were erased from the face of Halifax in the 1960s, victims of concrete and brick postmodern urban renewal. It was in there, amid what are now seemingly endless rows of offices and apart-ments, that Murphy ran. And it was in there that he found Shehan and Power. I look for a long time at the modern towers, trying to imagine the nineteenth-century character, trying to imagine Murphy speaking with Power and Shehan. Mostly, my efforts fail. Still, I manage to gain some sense of the scene and turn back, heading toward the Waterloo site, just past the Old Town Clock. There, I sit again on the grass, in view of the Waterloo, and imagine the unfold-ing scene as Shehan and the watchmen arrive.

"Well, it took us some minutes to go up," Shehan says. "I found a sailor leaning against the second step of the southern side of the northern stair. His head was on the step. I think he was dead. Murphy wished me to go for a doctor. I thought there was no life in Allen and instead went for the magistrate. Murphy went for a doctor."

Throughout his memory of the night, Shehan is interested only in the facts, in keeping order. Only once in all his recollections does he offer an opinion, which was this: "It appeared to me," Shehan said, "that if the sailor had jumped out of the window pointed out, he would not be lying in the position he was." Shehan's point was an important one that would be repeated by others at the scene. Maurice Power, Shehan's partner, made the same observation – and more.

From what little evidence we have of Maurice Power, he was the junior partner of the two watchmen, always following just a step behind Shehan. Perhaps for that reason, I imagine Power as smaller and thinner than Shehan. But in contrast to Shehan's words, the cadence of Power's words suggest a man who gave much thought to what he saw. "It was about a quarter to twelve when we were called by Murphy," Power remembers. "The man was sitting with his back against the balustrade of the bottom of the north staircase, about a gill of blood near him. I thought he was dead when I saw him. His head was laying on his shoulder. I felt it. There was no palpitation of the heart, and so I said, 'This man is dead.'"

The two watchmen looked carefully about the scene, Shehan noting, "It was a damp night. There was some broken glass thrown out of Sarah Myers' room while I was there. The glass was thrown out when we first went up. A woman, likely enough Myers, was look-ing out of the window. I then saw the sailor's hat, handkerchief, and cap. I left the body and went to see Alderman Morrisey. He referred me to Mr. Clarke, who accompanied me to the spot."

The offhand comment about the glass being thrown from Myers' window becomes stranger still in Power's description. "As I was stand-ing by the dead man's side," remembers Power, "Myers was throwing glass out of the window, and I abused her for doing so, and she laughed. I remarked on her conduct, in laughing over a dead body. When I went back to the body, and put my hand on his forehead, the head fell back as if he was dead. I did not raise the body till we lifted it on Shehan's back."

Why, I wondered, would Myers throw glass from her window, the same window from where the sailor was said to have jumped? Power offers his own sense of disconnect about the scene. "I think it would be impossible," he says, "that a man could have fallen out of the southern window and crawled to the northern steps. After Murphy called us, he went to Mrs. Ward's [Murphy's mother] and told her that a man had fallen out of the window. Her house was south of Murphy's. He threw some gravel up to the window to wake her. Murphy said, 'Oh Mother! There is a man-o-war sailor fell from Sarah Myers' window.' She answered, 'My God, how did it happen?' Mrs. Ward came to the house before we left to carry away the body. She went into the taproom door."

Another firsthand observation of the scene outside the Waterloo Tavern comes from a shipmate of Allen's, a man named James Baldwin. He remembers the night well. "I was a mariner on board Her Majesty's ship *Cumberland* in September 1853," he says. "I knew Alexander Allen. I had known him for two years before that period. He was a very sober industrious, steady young man. I never saw him worse for drink. He was about four or five and twenty years of age.

"I recollect the night he lost his life," continues Baldwin. "I first saw him between the hours of six and seven at the Waterloo Tavern, Thomas Murphy's place. Allen had some ginger beer, and I had some ale. He left the house, and I stayed. I next saw him a little before ten o'clock, at the corner of the Dog and Duck. It is a shanty well known and kept by Abraham Provost. He went in. I saw him no more until he was dead.

"I was going along one of the streets. Somebody hailed me and said, 'For God's sake go up to the Waterloo. One of your men has been killed.' I received the intimation of my comrade's death about a quarter past twelve o'clock. I know this because they sup at the Wellesley, where I was staying, at twelve o'clock, and they were just sitting down to supper when I left. I went up, thinking there had been a row, and would be a crowd, but I saw no person till I got up the stairs, when I saw a policeman. A black fellow [David Parsons] held a light to Allen's face. Allen was sitting in an upright position facing the street, his head resting against the fifth or sixth step, on the southern side of the north steps. A light was thrown on his face. He had a cut down both temples – the heaviest was on the right temple where the blood was congealed. The cut looked as though it had been inflicted by a sharp instrument. The black boy and the policeman told me he had fallen out of the south window. If he had fallen out of that window, I do not believe he could have been found in that posture. I aided Shehan in carrying the body down to the Police Office. We found his hat, cap, shoes and stockings lying beside him. They looked as if they had been thrown out.

"I went into the Waterloo. I saw Mary Anne Cole [another woman of the house] there. I might have been there about ten minutes before the body was removed. Murphy was not there at that time. I asked Mary Cole how it was done. She said he jumped out of the window. She was crying. I did not take particular notice of the cuts, because I was too much excited."

Baldwin's description gives me the first sense that the corpse had been a living person – twenty-four years of age, industrious, a modest drinker. Baldwin's tale fleshes out the events already described, but it also provides one interesting lead. Power also remembers Mary Anne Cole, but he makes no mention of her crying. "I went into the taproom," says Power. "The coloured chap, Parsons, and Mary Cole were there."

Why, I wonder, was Mary Cole crying?

One final witness provides me with some details and a corroborating opinion about the placement of Allen's body. City clerk James S. Clarke, whom Shehan had retrieved after he had first observed Allen, recalled this: "I was awakened on the night of the 7th September by a watchman. I got up and accompanied him to the Waterloo Tavern. It was quite a calm night, but overcast. I do not recollect whether it was raining. At the Waterloo, I found there a man lying on the ground, his head resting on a platform between two flights of steps, on a small board passed two or three inches from the ground, his feet extending towards the west and head inclining to the side. I thought the best course was to the [Police] Office. Shehan took him on his back and carried him down."

Behind me, I realize that sun was setting over Citadel Hill, slowly bleeding orange and red into the clouds. Tired, I decide to call it a day. Again, I place my pen, my map, and my notebook back into my shoulder bag. I stand, pull on my Red Sox cap, and wonder: was it possible that Alexander Allen had been alive after he hit the ground? Was it possible that he crawled a few feet before dying? The witnesses didn't think so. That, or they didn't consider the possibility. Why was the prostitute, Sarah Myers, behaving so strangely? And why was Mary Anne Cole crying?

It appeared that there was much more to the story.

With the whole scene replaying in my mind – the body falling from the window; Murphy, Gordon, and Parsons discovering the body; the watchmen, the mariner, the prostitute, the elderly mother standing over the body; Shehan walking with the body draped over his shoulder, one block north to George Street and then seven blocks east to the Police Station – I walk in the other direction, up and over Citadel Hill toward home and decide that tomorrow I will pick up the mystery's trail at the site of the old Police Office, and witness the arrests back at the Waterloo Tavern.

Meantime, I would consider the rhythm of this old city in the Golden Age of Sail.

Chapter 4

The City

The Cock-Up Theory of human history argues that our collective past is simply the sum of important people's blundering errors and endless inadequacies. This idea is also called the Theory of Cleopatra's Nose, which argues that Cleopatra's prominent prow so enticed the Roman leader Marc Antony that he lost track of business back home and allowed the Roman Empire to fall into chaos. I find myself steeping in this confused confluence of layman's historiography as I leave my house sometime before eight o'clock, under a cloudless morning sky. I ponder both theories, the Cock-Up and Cleopatra's Nose, interweaving them in the mundane, and not-so-mundane, details of a real Victorian murder-mystery, those accidental events that led to the horrible death of Alexander Allen and also led me to hunt for his possible killer 150 years after the fact.

Sipping at my silver enviro-mug filled with strong, black coffee, I stroll lazily across the Halifax Commons, west of Citadel Hill. This common land was once a rolling pasture for grazing sheep and agitated citizens escaping the grinding thrum of the city. Today, the Commons encompass a vast green space of public walking paths and baseball diamonds. I kick up the dust in one of those ball fields, remembering that, during the late Victorian Age, the sport of baseball – that new American creation out of Cooperstown, New York – was wildly popular here. Local teams like the Wanderers and the Resolutes drew great crowds to admire the local play. Baseball was so popular, in fact, that some years later the great Bambino himself, Babe Ruth, felt it worth travelling to Halifax on a goodwill tour after his retirement to have a few drinks at the local pubs and swat a few baseballs over a ball field near the Commons.

I imagine the overweight and over-liquored Sultan of Swat, standing in the dirt near home plate, swinging his pine bat at gently lobed balls. And as I walk past the fenced-in fountain at the Commons' centre, I imagine one of his hit balls flying through the air and imagine the assembled crowds cheering. The imaginary baseball lands ahead of me in the grass and rolls to a stop. Passing it, I look across the Commons to a row of Victorian-era houses across North Park Street. The thick moldings and multipaned windows return my attention to the Victorian Age and to the Golden Age of Sail, and I ponder the city and its people once again.

The evening before, I'd thumbed through my notes of the 1851 Halifax Census. These dry numbers give some rough sense of the city and of the people who occupied it. Of a total population of about 18,000, 3,668 were heads of families in the city's six wards, while 2,087 males and 2,974 females under the age of ten played in the streets and cried in their cribs. There were 2,911 children who attended the fifty-five schools of the city, including the Halifax Grammar School, the city's first school, located on the corner of Barrington and Sackville Streets. There were 1,211 males and 2,170 females between the ages of twenty and thirty clamouring for jobs and social position, most settling for modest survival. The disproportionate numbers of females to males in this age group suggests the sea and the military absorbed many of the restless and unemployed. So too, there were 1,388 males and 1,636 females between the ages of thirty and forty who settled down to the rhythm of Halifax life, some married, some not. And there were 1,058 males and 1,087 females between the ages of forty and fifty years of age who grew older, a few grew richer, but most just grew hardened to the difficulties of life in mid-Victorian Halifax.

Of those older than fifty, there is no mention, which may also suggest much about their hardships.

Of all these people, 6,166 people were married. Some 204 were widowers, and 760 were widows. So too, 395 people were deemed paupers. Eight males and two females were said to be deaf and dumb. Nine males and nine females were listed as blind. Lunatics numbered twenty-four males and thirty-two females; idiots just three males and three females. (No explanation was provided as to the difference.) Of "Indians" living in the city, there were said to be none. But "Colored Persons" – African-Canadians – numbered 382 males and 545 females, many living on the shores of Bedford Basin at the north end of the Halifax Peninsula, in what came to be called Africville.

Some twenty-seven clergymen ministered to the city, while twenty-four doctors cared for the sick and infirmed. There were 491 farmers who scratched out a living on the thin layer of dirt that blanketed the enormous face of stone stretching beneath the city, and 1,484 mechanics or craftsmen who shoed horses, made tools, crafted barrels, built homes, and stitched shoes. Some 681 merchants and traders, whose warehouses still sit on the Halifax waterfront, enriched the city as the Golden Age of Sail expanded. And just nineteen fishermen called Halifax their home, though 190 men, perhaps dockworkers or itinerant sailors, were "engaged at sea." Still, these numbers feel little more than dry facts, caricatures of people without meaning or context.

Halifax in 1843, the year the Old Cemetery was shutting its gates to time, was a city rapidly growing, rapidly changing, and rapidly emerging as an economic giant. The Golden Age of Sail for this city by the sea brought great fortunes and much optimism for the future. Yet, this wild growth paradoxically planted the seeds of its own demise.

Still crossing the Commons, I look at the houses along streets called Creighton, Agricola, Gottingen, and Maynard – houses built for the working classes of the mid-to-late 1800s – houses that still hint at the city's Victorian past. I stop beside an oak tree, at the edge of North Park Street, and sit. From my bag, I remove my notebook and carefully review three firsthand observations of the city.

In 1842, just one year after the incorporation of Halifax as a city, the fourteen-year-old heir to the Molson Brewery fortune, Jacky Molson, travelled to Nova Scotia from Quebec. "We anchored at Pictou at 2 a.m. Monday," writes Molson in his diary, "so we remained on board till the morning. We came down to Pictou in a ferryboat and went to the Stage Office to take our places in the stages. Instead of bringing stages with six horses, they brought two wagons. We were very uncomfortable for we had no place to put our feet at the bottom of the cart, it being filled up with baggage. Before we had been long on the journey it began to rain. We arrived at Truro at 7 p.m. and had a dinner, which was very acceptable to us poor half-drowned rats. We would have been glad to rest ourselves but that was impossible for fear of being too late for the [steamship] *Britannia,* which was to sail from Halifax on the following day."

Today, Truro, Nova Scotia, is just an hour's drive west of Halifax, along Highway 102, mostly through forests and rolling farmlands. I muse that this country scenery is little more than window dressing, now. The tangible sense of slow travel that Molson describes – the rain and the mud – is lost to modern travellers, enveloped as they are by air-conditioning and world-wide satellite radio signals. They only glance now and again out the passenger window at bemused cows and single-storey, cement strip malls to break the monotony.

That said, young Jacky Molson was riding the edge of technological change as he arrived in Halifax. On the heels of travel by slow horse and carriage, Jacky Molson was about to board the *Britannia*, the first of Nova Scotia's Samuel Cunard's steamship liners, travelling from Europe to Canada and back again. The *Britannia* and her sister ship the *Unicorn*, both built in 1840, were the harbingers of a new industrial age. On May 30, 1840, when the *Unicorn* arrived in Halifax from Liverpool, three thousand Haligonians – about one-fifth of the entire city's population – celebrated the event, filling the wharves, firing cannons, and waving flags. The steamship *Britannia* followed the *Unicorn* in July of 1840. And then in quick succession that year, Samuel Cunard launched the *Acadia*, the *Caledonia*, the *Columbia*, and the *Hibernia*. Through 1853, ten additional ships were built. Cunard's fleet may well have grown still if it hadn't been for the call of war. As per Cunard's ship contracts, the British government commandeered many of his ships in 1853, at the start of the Crimean War, the same year of Alexander Allen's death, for troop transport and the movement of war goods. By the time the war ended, Cunard found himself in competition with at least two other steamship lines, one from New York City and one from Liverpool. For Halifax, the safe economic transition of sail to steam was no longer secure.

Ironically, young Jacky Molson unwittingly hints at this shifting age. "As we passed along, on the road we saw the remains of a canal," he writes in his diary. "It was a most foolish undertaking and turned out in the ruin of many who invested their money in the stock. The most ridiculous part of it was their importing granite from Scotland for building the locks, although there was granite in Nova Scotia. If it was for some public building it would have been a different matter, but for canal locks it was the height of imprudence and extravagance."

The Shubenacadie Canal was started in 1826 with the idea that a canal would provide economic uplift for the centre of the province and a trade route to the Bay of Fundy. However, constantly interrupted and challenged, construction ended in 1831 with the bankruptcy of the Shubenacadie Canal Company. In 1854, the Inland Navigation Company started construction again and managed to finish the canal in 1861. But by then the Shubenacadie Canal already seemed a project passed over by time. The canal was closed in 1870 when a number of bridges were built preventing larger boats from passing through. In many respects, the Shubenacadie Canal captured the fleeting moment of that age's economic possibility.

"In a short time we arrived at Dartmouth," continues Molson, "a small town on the side of the harbour opposite to Halifax. And just as we got to the wharf one [of] the wheels of the larger wagon broke in pieces, and there we received the pleasing intelligence that the *Britannia* had not arrived. We crossed over to Halifax in a ferry where we arrived at half past two and immediately put up at the City Hotel, a new building not quite finished, conducted by Messrs. Parker and Rice. It is built of wood and at the back is shingled all the way up to the roof, which when neatly executed looks very well and I was told that it was much warmer than clapboarding."

Likely, the "City Hotel" Molson wrote about was the Halifax Hotel, built that year, in 1842, with the expectation of European tourists delivered to Halifax via the Cunard steamships. However, like the Shubenacadie Canal, the fortunes of the Halifax Hotel rose quickly and fell sharply. The European tourists never materialized, and hopes for their arrival faded as time passed. By 1849, the Halifax Hotel was bankrupt.

Still, in 1842, this new hotel spoke of optimism. "It is four stories high facing the street and five in the rear," Molson writes. "On the first floor are the following rooms: Grand Dining Room, a Ladies Ordinary, the Gentlemen's and Ladies' Drawing Rooms, a Smoking Room and a Reading Room. There is also a Bar Room where refreshments can be obtained. The hotel is traversed by three pair of stairs from top to bottom. It has a platform on the top commanding a most delightful prospect of all the shipping and the city."

After Molson looks about this island of optimism and comfort, he explores the city. "There is a peculiar custom prevalent [in the city] – that of building flats on the tops of houses," writes Molson. "Whether it is of any other use than that of a promenade for walking on in the summer evenings, I do not know. I think it is very dangerous in case of a chimney taking fire for it would very quickly reach the wooden flat and the house would be burnt. It so happened when I was at Halifax, the chimney of the Government House took fire and immediately communicated to the flat on the top of the roof and if immediate assistance had not been procured, this fine building must ere long have been a smoldering heap of ruins. There is another peculiarity in this city that I have not noticed in other cities that of having pumps in the streets. I dare say it is a great convenience to the people having fresh water so near to them but they could not do without them for the water of the harbour is salt. They are of great use in case of fire."

I look up and watch the pedestrians, most with backpacks or shoulder bags, as they stride across the Commons toward downtown. As they pass, I consider Molson's observations about the risks to a city built of close-set wooden buildings. His fears were well placed. For much of the nineteenth century only a modestly outfitted group of volunteer fire departments provided a defense against fire. And that defense, by most accounts, was shoddy. Serious fires in 1850 in the North Barracks, in 1857 along on Hollis Street, and most dramatically in 1859 on the north end of Granville Street forced the city to invest in better equipment, a proper water supply, and the use of brick and stone for buildings downtown. Still, despite all this, the city did not engage a full-time fire department until the late 1890s.

A breeze rustles the paper of my notebook. Distracted, I reach for my cup of coffee, take a sip, and then return to Molson's journey.

"While I was walking one evening on one of the roads heading to the country," Moslon continues, "I passed a brewery and distillery, situated towards the mouth of the harbour, belonging to a Scotsman called John Oal, who very kindly invited us in to see his establishment. He manufactures rum and whiskey, porter, ale, peppermint shrub and ginger beer.

"I afterwards went to see the Museum. It is in a stone building built of free stone. It contains several curiosities consisting of beasts, birds, fishes, insects and all other animals stuffed. They had some Indian curiosities such as spears, wooden axes and other weapons. The spear consists of a straight piece of hard wood made very smooth, to one end of which is attached a piece of bone sharpened at one end and rising with a slope exactly like the end of a fishhook. There was likewise an Indian wooden hatchet made of ironwood used by the South American Indians. There was large bone, which was found in Prince Edward's Island about four feet long and weighing about two hundred-weight, supposed to be the thigh-bone of some large animal that existed before America was discovered. But the best and most deserving of attention of the works of art was a small pair of scissors about one-eighth of an inch in length & weighing only one-twentieth of a grain; they are made of steel and manufactured at Sheffield (England)."

Molson's visit to the museum captures something of the growing Victorian Age's desire to organize and categorize. This new age of self-improvement and collective industry required a corresponding progressive history – human and natural.

Also in 1842, travelling from Liverpool to Boston on the same

Cunard steamship, *Britannia*, famed novelist Charles Dickens visited Halifax, after which he published a brief record of the experience. I look through my papers and find the quotation. Of Halifax, Dickens writes, "The town is built on the side of a hill, the highest point being commanded by a strong fortress, not yet quite finished. Several streets of good breadth and appearance extend from its summit to the water-side, and are intersected by cross streets running parallel with the river. The houses are chiefly of wood. The market is abundantly supplied; and provisions are exceedingly cheap. The weather being unusually mild at that time for the season of the year, there was no sleighing: but there were plenty of those vehicles in yards and by-places, and some of them, from the gorgeous quality of their decorations, might have 'gone on' without alteration as triumphal cars in a melodrama at Astley's. The day was uncommonly fine; the air bracing and healthful; the whole aspect of the town cheerful, thriving, and industrious. I carried away with me a most pleasant impression of the town and its inhabitants and have preserved it to this hour."

I am struck that both Dickens and Molson, like so many tourists excited by what is new and different, draw out the positive in what they saw. That said, they do capture something of the city's enthusiasm and optimism in the Golden Age of Sail.

Perhaps more clear-eyed, Robert Everest also described the city a decade later in his book, *A Journey Through the United States and a Part of Canada* (1855). In his description, Everest evokes the changing tide of history, as the old garrison town slips away to the new city brought to heel by Victorian mores. "The houses of Halifax appear slovenly kept and dirty," Everest writes, "nor when in the suburbs did I see a trace of the neat flower gardens I should have expected from people of English descent. Halifax is a great place for the army and navy; and whether the example of a life of idleness and amusement, balls and horse races, parties and gossiping, be, or not, prejudicial to the sober and business habits of a mercantile community, it is impossible to say. Certain it is that the newspapers complain grievously of the quantity of drunkenness and prostitution; and in this respect the place resembles ... other garrison towns of England."

I consider that the "slovenly kept and dirty" houses Everest writes about are all but gone from the city centre now, bulldozed in the name of urban renewal and economic progress. Even here, at the northern edge of the old city, the past ten or twenty years has seen the young, upwardly mobile, urban professionals purchase these old Victorian working-class homes for renovation.

Renovation with extreme prejudice.

On these old homes, these postmodern urbanites have imposed a narrow, historically amnesiatic dark vision of futurism: endless right angles, floating staircases, and leaking skylights. As a consequence, the remaining vestiges of Halifax's nineteenth-century character has steadily been stripped away. Old porcelain sinks and thick window moldings have been tossed out in favour of stainless steel stoves and colourful curved counter tops. In the modern age, it's better to remove useless, coal-burning fireplaces for sixty-five-inch shelving units designed for plasma televisions and multi-disc DVD players.

Ain't urban renewal grand.

As I finish my coffee, I remember that I have a body to follow. So I put my notebook back in my bag, stand, and start on my journey again. I cross North Park Street and walk slowly south along a row of houses painted in bold colours, toward the corner of Citadel Hill. There, I climb the western slope, following a paved road around the top, taking in the view – downtown Halifax and the harbour out to George's and McNab's Islands, all under a brilliant blue sky. Then I descend along the southeast side of the hill, arriving back on the corner of Brunswick (old Barrack) and Sackville Streets, just below where I'd sat on the grass the day before.

I again look across the street, a block to my left, and recall the Irish watchman, John Shehan, lifting the body of Alexander Allen onto his shoulder with the help of the mariner, John Baldwin. I watch Shehan carry the body down Barrack Street one block to George Street. Next to him walks James Clarke, the city clerk; the black servant, David Parsons; the petty thief and carpenter, John Gordon; and the Waterloo tavern-keeper, Thomas Murphy. I follow a few steps, and 150 years, behind, imagining the group moving in silence.

Along Brunswick Street, I stop at the top of what was George Street, below one of the oldest structures in the city, and certainly the most recognizable, the Old Town Clock. Even with the body over his shoulder, John Shehan almost certainly looked up and noted the hour.

I look at it now.

Erected at the turn of the eighteenth century by Prince Edward, the Duke of Kent, the Old Town Clock was a product of the Prince's time as Commander-in-Chief of His Majesty's Forces in Nova Scotia. This prim, punctual soldier-prince wanted a community clock for everyone in the city to see – and to provide a conspicuous timepiece against any excuse for being late. Unfortunately for the Prince, he had left for England by the time his clock was completed on October 20, 1803. Soon thereafter, the clock became the iconic symbol of the city and the inspiration for at least one bit of dodgy poetry, penned by no less than Nova Scotia's own Joseph Howe. In my notebook, I have scribbled one of the verses.

To The Town Clock

Thou grave old Time Piece, many a time and oft
I've been your debtor for the time of day;
And every time I cast my eyes aloft,
And swell the debt—I think 'tis time to pay.
Thou, like a sentinel upon a tower,
Hast thou still announced "the enemy's" retreat,
And now that I have got a leisure hour,
Thy praise, thou old Repeater, I'll repeat.

Howe was no Dante. But his poem does suggest something of the clock's place in the city's consciousness only fifty years after being built. That said, and though it may well represent a fine example of Georgian architecture rare in North America, the clock reminds me of an unimaginative wedding cake.

I turn away from the clock and head down what was the top end of George Street, following Shehan toward the old Police Office site.

This part of old George Street has suffered the same fate as Barrack and Albemarle – it was renamed. The city changed the name in 2000 because city council members, noting that the street was cut in two by the Grand Parade, felt a split street caused confusion for the city's citizens and visitors. Of course, that this end of the street had been safely called George for a quarter of a millennium, and that no one was particularly upset by the fact that it was called George on both sides of the Grand Parade for a quarter of a millennium, didn't stop this nonsensical act of civic 'progress' from taking its course. And so, the west end of George Street became Carmichael Street, in honour of Kate Carmichael, a city activist who later died of leukemia in 2001.

While turning from Brunswick (once Barrack) Street onto Carmichael (once George) Street and walking down to Market (once Albemarle) Street, I try to imagine the old shingled homes and stone buildings that once stood here. But my imagination fails in the face of a thick concrete and red brick multi-use Sportsplex and World Trade Centre on my left and a five-floor hotel and box-shaped restaurant on my right. It's only when I arrive at the Grand Parade, where George Street now begins, that I am offered some tangible hint of the city's past again.

A large rectangular area of paved parking, grassy knolls, and granite monuments, the Grand Parade was, and remains, the old city centre. At one end of the Grand Parade stands the City Hall, a sandstone, late-Victorian building, once the site of Dalhousie University. At the other end sits St. Paul's Church, the oldest place of Protestant worship in Canada and the first church in Halifax. In fact, St. Paul's Church is the oldest building in the city. I stop for a moment and admire its facade. It was built in the summer of 1750, designed to mimick St. Peter's Church in Vere Street, London, England, which had been designed by James Gibbs, a pupil of Sir Christopher Wren, architect and builder of London's St. Paul's Cathedral. In 1812, a north front and steeple were added, with two side wings in 1868, and finally a new chancel in 1872.

Sitting on a curb near the church, I look left across the Grand Parade and see fifteen or twenty people – tourists and bankers, businessmen and beggars. One enterprising young man strums on a sticker-covered guitar. At his feet, a guitar case is open for donations. He sings out of tune, but seems blissfully unaware of it – or maybe he doesn't care. Three other people, two men and a woman all dressed in denim and leather, relax on the east side of the Parade, smoking pot and chatting. On the cement walk in front of me, a man in a brown suit rushes by. He looks at his watch as he heads toward George Street and the waterfront. In the Grand Parade centre, a father and two children pose in front of City Hall while a mother takes a photo. To the right of the family, a young girl in shorts tosses an orange ball to her chocolate lab. The dog snatches the ball as it rolls and then races back to the girl.

The young traveller, Jacky Molson, walked through here as well in 1842. "On Sunday the 23rd of May, went to church at Halifax," he write in his diary. "The walls were erected at the expense of Government in 1750 and were made of wood. All the interior was at the expense of the congregation. At the altar upon black boards in gilt letters are the Lord's Prayer, Ten Commandments, and Creed besides which there were several tablets."

I resist the urge to go inside and instead head east, passing by the young girl and her dog, and exit the Grand Parade. I cross Barrington Street and continue east toward the water along George Street. At the corner of George and Granville Streets, I am again confronted with Halifax's past and present. To my right, inside a stone wall and iron fence, is historic Province House, where the provincial legislature sits. In the grounds, at its side, a statue commemorating the Boer War stands, a cast-iron soldier atop a granite platform, a gun raised above his head. Next to the monument stands the sandstone legislature, where the trial of Thomas Murphy for the death of Alexander Allen was held.

I continue walking east, looking left at Hollis Street, then up at the imposing bank towers – the Canadian Imperial Bank of Commerce and the Bank of Montreal, rectangular boxes of glass and steel, unimaginative phallic symbols to the power of money. Bigger is better, I guess. These buildings and their like have consciously displaced the steeples of churches, once the tallest buildings in the city, to provide new houses of worship for the post-industrial age. Looking at these twin towers of modern commerce and the two sandstone edifices of Victoria's reign – the Provincial Legislature and the Art Gallery of Nova Scotia – I imagine bookends of local Industrial Age history, from one age of Empire to another.

I am reminded that, as these buildings were conceived and constructed, the emerging Industrial Age brought with it industrial infrastructure. In March of 1840, the Halifax Gas Light and Water Company Act was passed, and by 1843, the first homes in Halifax were lit with gas. In December 1846, the Halifax City council deliberated the value of hydrants to combat fire: "The City Council met on Wednesday, and after a good deal of talk and noise, which with them is always the precursor of business, passed the following Resolution, 7 to 6: *Resolved* That it be intimated to the Water Company, that the City Council are willing to take charge of any number of fire plugs which they may be prepared to hand over, and to be a charge against the city from that period, at the rate set forth in their letter, but not to be paid for until the hydrants and fire plugs are put into operation, and the number of hydrants and fire plugs contemplated in the City completed."

In February of 1847, the House of Assembly made plans for modern communications, a telegraph line between Halifax and Toronto. Meantime, Cunard's ships had already made Halifax the temporary nexus of North Atlantic information. In April of 1846 the "largest mail ever received at the Boston Post Office, was brought there from the *Caledonia* [from Halifax] yesterday at half past one, P.M., consisting of 113 bags of letters and papers. It was important to forward the letters and papers for the South by the steamboat mail, which closes at 4 P.M. The clerks went at it, and before half past four o'clock, the mail for the South was on its way to New York! In less than three hours mail containing over 35,000 letters were sorted and dispatched by the clerks of the Boston Post Office."

Two years later, in February of 1849 from the spot now occupied by the Art Gallery of Nova Scotia just a few feet from me, Halifax began its "horse express" or "express," later becoming the "pony express." The local newspapers reported the first "express" this way: "A little after eight o'clock on Thursday evening last, the steamer

Commodore, Capt. Brown, arrived from Digby Basin, bringing Mr. Craig, an American gentleman, who had undertaken on behalf of the Associated Press of Boston and New York to express the news by the Steamer *Europa*, from Halifax to Saint John, and thence by Electric Telegraph to Boston and New York. The arrangements on the road from Halifax to Granville Point, were very complete, and the distance was accomplished with single horses, in a light sleigh, in eleven hours, being a speed of about thirteen miles an hour! The *Europa* arrived at Halifax on Wednesday afternoon at five o'clock, in eleven days from Liverpool, and on Thursday morning at four, the messenger with her news was at Granville Point, but owing to the unusual quantity of ice in Digby Basin, it was nearly four o'clock in the afternoon before the *Commodore* was got into clear water. On her arrival in Saint John the Electric wires were immediately set to work, and the operator here, Mr. Mount, transmitted the intelligence in a manner which, while it gave satisfaction to the American editors, proved that the management of the Office has been entrusted to very competent hands."

The second pony express run came in March of 1849 and was described this way: "The two riders galloped out of Halifax immediately after the arrival of the Cunard steamship *America,* at a speed 'unprecedented in this country.' *America* had arrived at the Halifax wharf at 2:30 a.m. on March 8th, 1849. The couriers arrived at Victoria Beach only three minutes apart, at 11:30 a.m., having taken 8 hours for the trip from Halifax (these are the times given in contemporary reports, which appear to allow about a half-hour to get the mail packages off the ship and handed over to the riders). This was early March, when the nights were still long, and the riders galloped at least as far as Mount Uniacke in darkness, with no light other than that provided by the stars and the Moon. On March 8th, 1849, the Moon reached full phase about 9 p.m. Halifax time. When the riders started from the Halifax waterfront, the Moon's phase was only 18 hours short of being full; for practical purposes they had the light of a Full Moon if the sky was cloudless, or nearly so. We do not know what the sky was like that night — they may have had anything from bright moonlight to utter darkness."

In a sense, whether or not there was moonlight, the age itself seemed bright. On June 5, 1849, Halifax celebrated its centennial. "At dark, the Province Building, Dalhousie College, and the Engine House were brilliantly illuminated. The residence of R. Noble, Esquire, was surrounded with a temporary bower of Forest trees, and illuminated with gas. It shone conspicuously. The Government House was illuminated till after midnight. The residence of John Richardson, Esq., Granville Street, was brilliantly illuminated during the evening."

I continue walking east for another block where I reach the site of the old Police Office. Nothing of the building remains today. Instead, a pedestrian bridge vaults over Lower Water Street to the 'new' Law Courts. The bridge is a brick and cement blight, yet it is somehow a fitting entrance to the hideous architecture of the modern Law Courts. The bridge is something of metaphor: from the past to the present, from the site of old justice to the new. Yet nothing remains of the past to indicate such meaning, and so the metaphor is lost. Only the ugliness remains.

At the foot of the bridge, just in front of me, a small man with dark, leathery skin, dressed in a blue cap, blue coat, and blue jeans, sits crouched against the cement. In his hands, he holds a paper coffee cup. As people walk by, he holds the cup up, gently following the passing pedestrians, and quietly pleads for change. Again and again, people in tailored suits – businessmen, politicians, and lawyers who populate the area – pass by without looking at the empty paper cup or even the man, until finally, one young woman with a key card dangling around her neck stops. She reaches into her pocket, pulls out a closed fist, and drops change into the cup. The man says nothing, just looks to the next pedestrian passing by – me. Feeling the guilt I always feel in passing such people, I reach into my pocket, wrap my hand around the loose change, and drop it into the cup. The man looks at me briefly and nods. Then he looks to the next man in a suit who whisks by without a glance.

I leave the man with the paper cup and walk a few steps into a wedge of green space, flowerbeds, and stones that was once the site of the Police Office. There I sit at a wooden bench and pull from my bag some papers and my notebook. Among the papers, I find photocopied pictures.

Two are of the old Police Office, each taken from a different angle. One is taken just across the street from where I sit, looking up George Street to the Old Town Clock. The building that now holds the Art Gallery is familiar, but little else is. In the intersection of George and Water Streets, one two-wheeled cart with bundled sticks sits next to another cart, laden with wrapped goods. One cart is pulled by an ox; the other, by a man. Black gas lamps stand on the right side of the street. On the left side, I can just make out the entrance to the open-air Cheapside Market, now part of Bedford Row. A crowd walks south along the sidewalk, entering and exiting the market. Across the street from the market stands the Police Office. In this picture, I can only make out the first two windows of the east side and the slanted, shingled roof.

The second photograph is taken from the Cheapside Market, looking north. The market area is filled with shoppers and vendors, the vendors sitting in front of their wares laid out on the ground. A few have tables with vegetables. Across the street, a few feet from where I now sit, is the entrance of the Police Office. Built of brick, the police office building has a pitched roof with three large windows on the second floor. Below these, the entrance to the building has a double door with a rounded window just above it. The two windows on either side of the door are arched to mimic and balance the entrance.

In the early morning of September 8, 1853, it was through this arched doorway that the body of Alexander Allen was carried by the watchman, John Shehan. And it was from these doors that John Shehan, Maurice Power, and a policeman named Patrick Caulfield walked back up the hill to the Waterloo Tavern to make arrests.

Arrests on suspicion of murder.

Chapter 5

The Suspects

In the 1850s, Karl Marx called it the theory of philosophical materialism, but those who found his historical tool useful later called it historical materialism. Marx turned out to be a lousy prognosticator of inevitable class warfare and the utopian state to follow, but he did manage – just around the time of Alexander Allen's death – to craft a fine theoretical means for understanding history.

Marx recognized that the human process of creating stuff – food and tools, needs and comforts – was also the human process that created our social, cultural, and economic conditions. These conditions were the fundamental forces that shaped our relationships, particularly in an age when groups of people were engaged in the mass production of stuff. Marx called these groups, classes. But 'class' in his sense is best understood as a relationship rather than a thing. That is, you can't have a class of factory workers without a class of factory owners. Best to think of 'class' as the stuff that comes from the conflict between groups of people. Of course, history is further complicated by cultural experience, understanding, and expectation overlaid on the economic relationships. If nothing else, historical materialism seemed a more fruitful way of thinking about the past than picking at Cleopatra's Nose – better to choose Karl over Groucho.

While still sitting on an uncomfortable wooden bench in the small green space once occupied by the old Police Office, I think vaguely about Marx's philosophical materialism and about the context surrounding the murder of Alexander Allen. In one hand, I hold a large coffee, bought at a newspaper shop across the street to my left. And in my other hand, I hold a photocopy of a peculiar mid-Victorian picture, a pen and ink drawing from the early 1850s of the Cheapside Market, which was once just across the street from me to my right. I imagine the market – the chatter of the crowd walking among the vendor's wares; the sound of wooden wheels rolling along the uneven ruts; the smell of fresh vegetables, fish, and meats mixing with the salt air. Overhead, I see gulls circling and hear their calls. In front of me, an ox snorts while it strains to pull a cart laden with barrels up George Street.

I look down at the drawing in my hand. It is a close-up, a sketched scene dense with nearly twenty people. All but one are women. More than a dozen are white, and a half dozen are black. Three of the black women sit on stools, selling mayflowers from wide wicker baskets. These women look drawn, their faces weary. They all wear dresses of heavy cloth – dark, frayed, and patched – their heads covered with patterned kerchiefs tied in knots at the chin. One of the women wears a wide-brimmed hat. As with two other women in the picture, she smokes a corncob pipe from which the artist has drawn a long curl of smoke. The white women, inspecting the mayflowers, are all drawn with careful attention to their graceful movements, their chins up and their shoulders back. They are well-attired, wearing fashionable ankle-length dresses that billow out from their narrow waists. As well, they wear wide-brimmed hats replete with ribbons and flowers. Two carry ruffled parasols.

The picture fascinates me. In some senses, it captures the unique social, ethnic, and class relationships of the city – the relationships of the Africans, the Irish, and the English; of the rich and the poor. In the drawing, the artist makes clear his sense of the relationship among black women and white women. He is careful to juxtapose those who are selling at the curb's corner and those who are buying, those who have money to spend and those who do not, those who are smiling in the picture and those who are not. The drawing reveals a cross-section of a relationship's moment, one forged through mutual commerce, socialization, and experience. Though African slavery has for twenty years been outlawed when this picture was drawn, it is clear – at least among the wealthier classes of Halifax – that black women are subservient.

I look up and imagine the market again, imagine a wealthy English woman walking among the vendors' stalls. She inspects the mayflowers and then the vegetables, but she buys nothing. Further along, she picks up a wicker basket, turns it over, and runs her hand along the bottom. She looks at the vendor – a black woman sitting at the curb, smoking a pipe – and asks how much it costs. The vendor takes the pipe from her mouth and tells her. They gently haggle and finally money changes hands. Though I detect nothing in the tone of their voices, the relationship between the two women seems firmly set, collectively understood, with invisible lines of social decorum. Once the purchase is made, the wealthy woman turns from the vendor and walks on, basket in hand, and disappears into the crowd.

I look again at my picture. Though it does not reflect it, the same understanding of subservience is true for black men – and also for the city's Irish. The division of black and white was, in truth, a subdivision – or sub-diversion – of rich versus poor. And in Halifax the rich were largely English; the poor, Irish and Black. On Barrack Street, the relationship among these poor subgroups – the Irish and the blacks – was muddled, blurred by the common experience of poverty and the violence that came with it. Both the Irish and blacks suffered terribly under the oppressive, exploitive hand of the English for centuries – as tenant farmers and slaves. It was understandable that this three-way relationship was culturally and economically transplanted from the British Isles and other British colonies to Halifax at its founding.

What was new to this relationship in the 1850s was the Victorian Age's press against the perceived social backwardness of the lower orders. The hubris of an age that justified a brutal British Empire also justified the grinding downward pressure against those groups who felt the burden of poverty. This new industrial economy only reinforced the cultural English bias of superiority soon sold in the guise of science – giving us the absurdities of phrenology and 'race' and Social Darwinism. And, of course, the targets of this pseudo-science were the Irish and blacks. Certainly these underlying assumptions of superiority by the English over these groups shaped the character of Halifax. But, fundamentally, so too did these two ethnic groups.

Nearly 200 Irish settlers came ashore with Cornwallis in 1749. By 1752, another sixty-two Irish men and women arrived. By 1760, nearly one-third of the 3,000 people who lived in Halifax were Irish, and most of these were Catholic. The second great wave of Irish immigrants came in the mid-1830s. With its nearly hundred-year-old Irish community, Halifax was an attractive escape from the various troubles in Ireland. That said, these immigrants arrived in a city – as was the case in so many cities in North America – where Irish Catholics were hardly made to feel welcome. In Halifax, the toleration of the Irish immigrants was just that – mere tolerance. And this shaped the relationship for centuries. It is no accident that, more than 250 years after the founding of the city, even into the first decade of the twenty-first century, Halifax's two major city high schools – situated just two blocks apart – are called Saint Patrick's and Queen Elizabeth: a none-too-subtle symbol of the Irish Catholic and the English Protestant relationship in the city.

At the same time, the other fundamentally defining human reality of Halifax was its African population. Africans had lived in Nova Scotia from its earliest years, the first African, Mathieu Da Costa, arriving in 1605 as an interpreter for the then Governor de Mont. Da Costa, who it would seem had been to the area before, knew the Mi'kmaq language. A quarter century after Da Costa, Africans began arriving in Nova Scotia as servants for British colonists and then later as slaves for Loyalists fleeing the rebel American states. More Africans migrated north following the American Revolution, attracted by the promise of free land. But as with the Irish, Africans and people of African descent arrived in Halifax at its inception.

The slave population existed in Nova Scotia until 1833, when the British parliament ended slavery in all its territories. By 1848, the first land grant had been given on the north end of the Halifax peninsula, on the shores of Bedford Basin. This sub-community of Halifax was later called Africville. And as with the Irish community, the city's black community was poorly treated by the largely English civic leaders. Even as the city proper was growing and prospering with gas lighting, running water, and sewage, Africville was left to linger in the past. In the 1850s, the new Nova Scotian railway literally cut Africville in two, symbolically leaving the community behind as it passed through each day – never stopping.

As I look at the pen and ink drawing, I consider the faces of these black women, imagine their long walk into the city each day from the shores of Bedford Basin, imagine them setting up their wares in the Cheapside Market just across from me. I consider, too, that the servant at the Waterloo, soon to be accused of murder, David Parsons, was black. I see him walk through the Police Office door on that damp September night, Maurice Power, the watchman, recalling that Parsons "came down to the Police Office with his braces hanging down, his breeches' straps still hanging low from his waist."

Inside the building at the bottom of George Street, the policeman Patrick Caulfield sees the body of Alexander Allen coming through the door over the shoulder of John Shehan. "I saw the body when it was brought down to the Police Office," he remembers, "about half past twelve." City clerk James Clarke enters the office in front of him and escorts the body to a back room at the end of the hall, where it is laid on a table. Outside the room, David Parsons and John Gordon wait, uncertain and unnerved.

After ten or fifteen minutes, Thomas Murphy arrives with Dr. Jason Allan. Dr. Allan was awoken at his home on Argyle Street, a few blocks east and south of the Waterloo Tavern, by the sound of Thomas Murphy's fist thumping on his front door. "I was called at 12 o'clock on the 7th of September by Murphy," he remembers, "to see a man killed in Barrack Street. The evening was cloudy and dark. The ground was damp. However, the body was in the Police Court before I saw it there." As Dr. Allan and Thomas Murphy make their way to Barrack Street, they are stopped by an unidentified man and told that the body of Alexander Allen is in transit to the Police Office. So they change course and head east, to the waterfront.

When Dr. Allan arrives at the Police Office, he is escorted down the hall, past Parsons and Gordon, who sit restless on a bench. At the end of the hall, the door is open and Dr. Allan enters. Inside, James Clarke stands near the body. He is talking with Alderman Morrisey, who arrived just minutes before. Clarke and Morrisey nod at Dr. Allan, who removes his coat, places it on a chair, and approaches the table. "When the doctor came," says Clarke, "he applied his ear to the body, and said, 'It is all over, the man is dead.'"

Dr. Allan remembers that he "proceeded to look for life, but found none." "The body was cold," he says, "except about the regions of the heart." So he mentally notes that the sailor could not have been dead for more than an hour. He then reaches across Alexander Allen's shoulders. Dr. Allan turns "the body over" and hears "a small gurgle from the throat," whereupon the sailor's jaw "fell open." With the body on its side, Dr. Allan quickly examines the back, but finding nothing, he rolls the body down again, and then binds up the jaw with a strip of cloth.

He can do no more. He pulls on his coat and tells Morrisey and Clarke that he will perform an autopsy later that day. Then he leaves the room. Clarke follows Dr. Allan into the hallway. "I found Murphy sitting on one of the benches," says Clarke. "I told him to remain in custody. He said, 'Certainly, Sir.'" Clarke is surprised by Murphy's calm. "Murphy showed no indisposition to comply with my request," Clarke remembers. "He sat there quite quietly and did not appear at all anxious."

After talking with Murphy, Clarke knows what has to happen now; he knows the importance of gathering timely evidence before stories change and evidence disappears. Nearly ninety minutes have passed since the body arrived at the Police Office. "It may have been an hour and a half from the time of taking the body down," remembers the watchman Power, "till we made the arrests." Clarke is informed that Parsons and Gordon, uncertain about what to do while waiting, decide to return to the Waterloo. So Clarke immediately calls for Shehan, Power, and the policeman, Caulfield. "I sent the watchmen to arrest the other three," recalls Clarke, "and in a short time they returned with them."

In my imaginary market, the crowds are thinning now and the vendors pack up their wares. The black woman hands her remaining baskets to a grey-haired black man in a thick blue coat patched at the elbows. Without speaking, he takes the baskets from the woman and piles them carefully in a wooden handcart by his side.

While I watch, I think about David Parsons. Though he is called "boy" and "coloured" frequently throughout the testimony, it is unclear whether those who used the words were necessarily racist in the way we understand the term today. The prevalence of blacks in the Barrack Street social milieu suggests a more complex relationship than simply that of master and servant, white and black, rich and poor. Though described as "boy," Parson's testimony is well-regarded by the prosecution and the defense. From his testimony, it is clear that Parsons is thoughtful, articulate, and confident. Certainly, as I wince reading the words "boy" and "coloured," hearing them through modern ears, I also consider that David Parsons is treated as an equal, not by the civic leaders, of course, but by those who lived their lives on The Hill. It is an unfortunate trick of history that we often look at the past with modern hindsight and present-day biases. In doing so, we miss the nuance of certain relationships within the context of their age.

I keep this thought in mind as I watch the two watchmen and the police officer leave the Police Office front door and step onto George Street. I imagine that they cast a quick look south, at the quiet Cheapside Market, and then walk up the hill, toward the Old Town Clock – perhaps visible as a faint shadow in the darkness, if visible at all.

I stand and gather my things, then follow the three back up George Street, across the Grand Parade, and through Carmichael Street. Along the way I consider the rhythms of their movement. I try, without success, to imagine what they might be thinking. After fifteen minutes, I arrive at the entrance to my Rickard's Red pub. I consider going inside, but as it's not quite noon, I choose instead to make my way across Brunswick Street, north, half a block to the stairs leading to the Old Town Clock. There, I step off the wooden stairs onto the grass and cut across the face of the clock building. I find a comfortable spot overlooking the street and watch what was the Waterloo Tavern.

Shehan and Power take charge on entering the Waterloo by the north stairs. Inside the taproom, the three officers find John Gordon, David Parsons, Mrs. Ward, and another woman who worked at the Waterloo named Jane O'Brien, all seated. As policeman Patrick Caulfield remembers it: "I was sent by Alderman Morrisey and Mr. Clarke to bring down Gordon, the black boy, and Sarah Myers. They did not object to come. I did not like to ask any questions of the prisoners. When I went, Gordon was sitting in Murphy's room. Gordon said that he and Murphy had been writing an estimate when the man fell out of the window. I am positive that Gordon told me that they were drawing the estimate when the man fell out of the window." Caulfield's insistence hints at a disagreement about what was said at the Waterloo. "Gordon was going away from the house," Caulfield recalls being told, "but Mary Cole had asked him to stay till Murphy came back, not to leave her alone. I went up to the room the man was said to have jumped out of. The sash was not broken but the glass was. The lower half was out lying on the floor. I remarked how would a man deliberately take out the sash before jumping out. I did not examine the house to see if there was blood about. I looked more after the safety of my prisoners. I did not go upstairs that night. Shehan went up and brought down the prisoners. I stayed in the taproom."

"When I went back," remembers Shehan, "I asked for Myers and was told she was in Ballard's room. I can't say whether Myers' door was locked or not. I examined the room. There was no sign of blood in the entry of stairs or landing. The stairs are very narrow. I recollect that the steps pass a window. I went up first to Ballard's room and then by the back of the house and upstairs to Myers' room without going through the taproom. Myers showed me a basin of water and said, 'There is the water he was washing in.' I said there was no sign of blood. She said, 'The water was left with him. I don't know whether he washed in it or not.' I said he had not been up there because from the wounds on him I presumed he would have left blood behind him."

It was then that Shehan asked Jane O'Brien about Myers' whereabouts. As O'Brien recalls it, "I went up to Myers' room with the two watchmen. The window was put back in its place. There were four panes of glass broken. Myers put it back. I saw the man's clothes lying near him outside, but don't know who put them there. When I went down to the taproom, I saw Myers there intoxicated. She was agitated, but as she was in liquor I did not ask her any questions. The deceased had his shoes and stockings on when he went upstairs," O'Brien says. Then she adds this: "A person falling from Myers' window would fall upon the steps."

Power remembers much the same about the return to the Waterloo: "When I was sent to arrest him," Power said, "Gordon showed me a piece of paper that he said Murphy and he were writing at the time that the man fell out of the window. It was an estimate, something about sashes he was going to the country for. I told him I could do nothing about the paper."

Power notes that Murphy's mother, Mrs. Ward, was there as well. "She was there when I went up to arrest the other parties. Matilda Ballard and Sarah Myers were in bed together. Sarah Myers was not in her own room. Jane O'Brien was in the house. We asked for his shoes and they told us they were in the street, where we looked for and found them. We made the arrests upstairs. I found Sarah Myers's door locked. She unlocked it, after she got up to come with me. She was in bed with all her clothes on. She was not sober. She was drunk. I think Myers said she did not care about her sleeping in her room after a man had jumped out of the window. She took hold of Shehan's arm to go down to the Police Office."

Power and Shehan continue to look around, asking questions of Myers as they do. "There was no light in the room, out of which it was said the man had fallen," says Power. "Myers said she knew nothing about it, that she was in the taproom at the time. Ballard and O'Brien remained in the house while we took other prisoners."

Later, when asked about the letter from John Gordon, Maurice Power couldn't recall it. "I am sure I did not see the letter from Gordon, can't swear that he was doing work for Murphy."

Having found the people Clarke sent them to find, the watchmen and policeman gather together Ballard, Myers, Gordon, and Parsons and leave the Waterloo. None offer resistance, but Myers needs help.

Along the way down the hill, Power muses to his friend Shehan, "I remember a soldier falling down from the top of a house and walking away uninjured. He slid down the roof, dropped from the eves to the balustrade, and from there to the ground."

Shehan just nods.

After they arrive at the Police Office, Clarke begins his examination with Myers. "Sarah Myers was in a state of intoxication," he recalls.

Still, Myers has much to say. "I saw Allen, the deceased, for the first time this summer," she observes in short, slurred sentences. "He was in the taproom tonight, about 6:15 o'clock. He was a short time there and went out again. He came back about eleven o'clock or a little thereafter. His face was dreadfully cut over the eye and bleeding. He called for two glasses of brandy. He gave the rest to the coloured chap. He was talking at the bar with Murphy."

Here, Myers hesitates while Clarke waits for more. Uncomfortable, Myers looks at the floor, and then up again at Clarke. She sighs, then speaks. "Murphy said he had better go upstairs and the girls would give him water to wash," she continues. "He went upstairs with me. There was water in the basin upstairs and I told him to go and wash there. I don't know whether he washed or not as I went down for a pitcher of water. I am sure I was not upstairs at that time, a quarter of an hour or half an hour, but went into the room, and after pointing out the water basin to the man, immediately returned. I went downstairs then. I was not longer than a quarter of an hour. I was talking with Matilda."

When Clarke speaks with Gordon, the story is similar. Gordon claims to have resided at the Waterloo for three weeks. He claims to have been in the taproom at about 8:30 p.m., went out, and then returned about ten o'clock. He says he did not stop in the taproom when he returned, but rather went upstairs to his room. There, he undressed and went to bed. He didn't say whether he'd actually fallen asleep, but he did say he was "awoken by the noise of something falling." He jumped up and listened, but heard nothing, until Myers came running upstairs. "She went into her room," claims Gordon, "and called out 'My God, where is the man?'" Gordon said he had "observed the light which she carried shining under the door of my room as she passed." "I got up," he says, "and saw her pick up the sash of the window from the floor. It was torn from the window. I then went down to Murphy. There was nobody in the taproom, except the colored boy. I told the boy the man must have got out of the window for the sash was broken and the man was gone. On that Murphy came out of his own room, asked me what was the matter, and I told him. We then opened the front door, looked, and saw the man lying between the two flights of stairs. He went down, over-hauled him, and then ran for the watchman. I then went and dressed myself and came down again. I did not tell Shehan that I was writing with Murphy in the sitting room when the man fell from the window. Cole was in the room with Murphy when I came down."

At the inquest, a sober Myers disagrees with Gordon's version. "I did not go upstairs and pass Gordon's room with a candle," she says, "did not enter my room and call out 'good God, where is the man. He has jumped out of the window' – or words to that effect. I was going up with the water, in the entry, when Gordon came downstairs and told us that the man had leaped out the window. I then ran up the stairs. I saw the window out and several panes of glass broken. I had no candle with me, but left the candle in the room with the man, when I came down. I looked out the window and saw the man out in the street, lying with his back against the steps with his feet out into the street. I went downstairs again and found that Murphy had gone out, found the man, dead, and ran for the watchmen. I never said I went downstairs for a glass of brandy. Gordon came into my room, a few steps, after I went up and saw the man out of the window. He said, that man has fallen out of the window and killed himself, for I heard the sash fall when he went out.

"Gordon was in his own room. I never cohabitated with him.

Allen took off his shoes before I left the room, and I found his cap, handkerchief, and stockings in the room afterwards. I threw all these out of the window. I did not know what to do with them. No person spoke to me from the street below when I was chucking out the things, nor was any girl looking out of the window above me. Gordon had his trousers and shoes on when he came down.

"The fiddler, Shortis, played until eleven o'clock. There was not much dancing that night. I had been drinking but not so much as that I did not remember what happened. The black man told me he had got a glass from the man. The sash was not put into the frame until I went away with Shehan about two o'clock. Allen said my shipmates have beaten me awfully down in the next street."

Later that night, after Clarke interviews and arrests the suspects, the city jailor, James Wilson, receives Mary Anne Cole, the woman who had been crying when the sailor, James Baldwin, entered the Waterloo. She was still crying now. As Wilson remembers it, "I had a conversation with her about this trial. I said, 'Mary, has it come to this at last?' She burst out crying and said, "I had nothing to do with it. I was in Tom's room when they were upstairs killing the man.' The following day, she denied using this expression. I am confident, however, that these were the words she used."

In a flash of emotion, Mary Anne Cole offers a starkly different account of the evening's accidental events, a stunning counter-tale of murder. Quick as it is offered, however, it disappears in denials. But the damage is done. The carefully woven tale of a half dozen witnesses wildly unravels, and I am left wondering: what really happened that night?

With the afternoon wearing on, I stand in the shadow of Citadel Hill, with the Old Town Clock protecting me from a steady wind. The evidence of that evening, September 7 and into the early morning of September 8, 1853, is now more muddled, unclear, and contradictory. Alexander Allen's body in relation to the window, the whereabouts of Gordon before the death, the strange behaviour of Sarah Myers after the 'accident,' the missing blood from the washbasin in Myers' room, the confession and its quick retraction from Mary Anne Cole – all unresolved. Something happened at the Waterloo Tavern that night – but what? What was it that Cole said? "They were upstairs killing the man ..."

"Upstairs killing the man ..." I think to myself as I walk down the grassy slope to the set of stairs beneath the clock. From there, I make my way onto Brunswick Street, looking for a moment down George Street to the waterfront where, in the old Police Office, the body of Alexander Allen still lay. I then turn left and make my way home, still thinking about the unresolved questions.

Inside the Police Office, after watching John Gordon, David Parsons, Matilda Ballard, Sarah Myers, Mary Anne Cole, and Thomas Murphy brought to jail, James Clarke orders the body of the sailor be taken to the Poorhouse near Artillery Park. So, as the sun comes up, Alexander Allen's body is on the move again, up the hill, around the Grand Parade, over to Barrack Street, past the Waterloo Tavern, south into Artillery Park, and then a block west to the brick Poorhouse. It is there, just past noon on Thursday, September 8, that Dr. Allan undertakes a detailed autopsy.

It seems Alexander Allen still has something to say.

Chapter 6

The Dead

In 1842, German physiologist and physician, Carl Friedrich Wilhelm Ludwig put forward the radical Ludwig's Theory, which explained, in purely chemical and physiological terms, the simple function of the liver. Why was it 'radical'? Because most people at that time still believed that the liver had a mystical life force. Ludwig also put forward another theory that year that explained, to the latent medieval minds of the early Victorian era, the very wonder that was urine. Though they seem trifling now, Ludwig's Theory on the liver and his work on urine, medically and scientifically, were forceful leaps into the modern age of rational science.

That said, some forty years later, in 1889, the Testicular Extract Theory – posed by French-American physician Charles Edouard Brown-Sequard – posited that the injection of liquefied guinea pig testicle under the skin of an aged man would invigorate his sexual drive and prowess. Not surprisingly, the Testicular Extract Theory was discredited, though not before who knows how many injections were dispensed to willing human, well, guinea pigs.

Needless to say, medical science in 1853 was a curious mix of medievalism and modernism. In the *Novascotian* newspaper during

1853 and 1854, in issue after issue, I found this single column advertisement prominently announcing this cure-all:

Russia Salve Vegetable Ointment

Cures burns, cancers, sore eyes, itch, felons, scald
head, nettle rash, cuts, corns, scalds, rheumatism,
sores, flea bites, whitlow, ulcers, warts, sore nipple,
sties, festers, ringworm, scurvy, bunions, sore lips, in-
grown nails, spider stings, shingles, eruptions, mos-
quito bites, chilbains, frozen limbs, wens, sore ears,
boils, flesh wounds, piles, bruises, chapped hands,
sprains, swelled nose, eiysioelas, lame wrist. Bites of
venomous reptiles are justly cured by this excellent
ointment.

The nineteenth century brought theories that would utterly
reshape the science of the twentieth century – from Louis Pasteur's
pasteurization to Charles Darwin's theory of evolution to Sigmund
Freud's psychoanalysis. The transition in thinking was transforma-
tive. In the early Victorian Age, scientists believed in an odour-based
miasma theory to explain illness. But by the age's end, scientists
would understand bacteria as the cause of illness. At the end of the
age, the use of antiseptics and anesthetics changed medical practice
dramatically, but during its beginning – and in some cases throughout
– the ancient cures and practices still held sway. For example, many
at that time believed that babies were noxious carriers of infections
and disease, while crying infants were sometimes quieted with doses
of opium and alcohol.

Similarly, at the start of the age, crowded and unsanitary conditions in housing were not recognized as a health risk. Consequently,
diseases such as typhus, scarlet fever, influenza, and yellow fever were
a constant threat. In 1834, with congested housing and dismal sani-
tary conditions, Halifax suffered a cholera epidemic. In the first six
weeks of the outbreak, 762 were struck ill and 284 died. Ignorant of
the cause, scientists and doctors could only provide comfort. In the
end, only the cold weather slowed and finally stopped the spread.

I consider the scope of nineteenth-century scientific and technological change – of Louis Pasteur's scientific breakthroughs transform-
ing modern medicine and of Samuel Cunard's steamships making
obsolete the Age of Sail – as I make my way south, under a thick
blanket of grey clouds. I walk by the Waterloo Tavern site and pass
through the intersection of Brunswick and Sackville Streets along a
relatively new stretch of Brunswick that weaves its way to Spring
Garden Road, the busiest shopping stretch in Halifax. From there, I
walk west one block and then turn right onto Queen Street. A block
and a half north from there, I stop at the corner of Artillery Park and
look through the wrought iron fence into the grounds. Somewhere in
there, 150 years ago, the naked, bloodied body of Alexander Allen lay
on a baker's table in the Poorhouse, waiting for an autopsy.

Today, nothing remains of the Poorhouse, just a collection of
mid-century Victorian buildings maintained by the Canadian military. Still, these old red brick houses vaguely suggest something of the
time, providing a physical tapestry for my imagination. One particular building, looking older than the rest, stands just twenty feet from
me, facing onto Queen Street. I look at it, and then look at a small
hand-drawn map in my hand – a copy of a torn, yellowed 1851 Halifax city map. After orienting myself to the map, I look up again at
the building and at the surrounding grounds. If my map is correct,
this building was erected on the foundation stones of the old Poorhouse. I carefully examine it: one and a half floors, shingled sloping
roof, gabled windows, wooden double doors, and four-paned windows
painted white. The tarnished bronze plaque near to the door indicates that this building is the Cambridge Military Library. I try pic-
turing this place as the Poorhouse where the Alexander Allen autopsy
took place. But my effort fails. Feeling the need to sit, I decide coffee
might help my imagination.

So I walk back to the "newer" part of Brunswick Street, some
forty yards or so east of the Poorhouse, to a single level coffee shop
tucked between the Artillery Grounds and a folk-music store. Inside
the coffee shop, oversized flowers and foliage – blue irises and leafy
greens – are painted on terra cotta coloured walls, all vaguely sug-
gesting the Mediterranean on the North Atlantic. To the left of the

main counter, a large Art Deco analog clock wrapped in a single line of blue neon light tells me it's twenty past nine. I make my way to the counter, where I survey the multicoloured chalkboard offerings, and then stand patiently behind three customers waiting to place their order.

The place bustles with people, a university crowd mostly – lots of tattoos and nose piercing and some existential talk frequently punctuated with the word "like." With my shaved head and a week's growth of beard, I might actually fit in – if I were twenty years younger. That said, Michael Jackson's "I Want to Rock With You" chirps merrily from speakers attached to the ceiling, and I spy a few sets of platform shoes mixed among the Teva sandals and rubber-shoe Crocs.

I guess "old," is like, you know, the new "new."

The customers in front of me each wear white earphones attached to iPods hidden somewhere in their pockets. Listening to music faintly escaping from their earphones, they happily ignore everyone else around them as though conversation with a coffee-shop clerk or a stranger is an encumbrance in this new-wave world. When finally they do talk to the clerk, I bristle at the Latinate orders for "cappuccinos" and "lattes."

When I reach the counter, I order – perhaps a little loudly – a "straight black coffee, large." That's right, no lattes or cappuccinos here, thank you very much. I look around for a reaction to my minor act of linguistic java rebellion, but it goes utterly unnoticed – like an old man in a trendy coffee shop. So I turn back to the clerk, who fills my coffee cup and places it on the counter.

It's in a ceramic mug painted with a smiling blue sheep.

"Oh, God," I mumble.

Mildly embarrassed, I take my blue sheep mug and walk slowly to a small round table in the northwest corner of the shop. There, I put my coffee down and sit on a pine bench. Once I am comfortable, I look out the plate-glass window where I can just see, off a gentle curve in Brunswick Street, another old city graveyard, a bit of grass and tombstones next to the old Methodist Church. This small, forgotten cemetery remains the only physical reminder of what was in the immediate area in 1853. I find myself thinking that the old Methodist graveyard, like the city's first cemetery, was probably fenced off many years ago to keep in the ghosts.

I take a healthy sip of my coffee. It's pretty good – even with the blue sheep still smiling at me. I then put the mug down, open my bag, remove my notebook, and revisit the scene at the Poorhouse.

Just before midday on Thursday, September 8, 1853, after a few hours of restless sleep, Doctor Jason Allan makes his way from his Argyle Street home to the Poorhouse, six or seven blocks south and west. A two-floor, brick, Dickensian edifice, the Poorhouse is necessarily cold and unforgiving. Here, the aged and desperately poor go as a resort of last hope. But no hope resides here today – Alexander Allen's naked corpse lies on a baker's table, in the kitchen.

Dr. Allan walks through the front door carrying a black and brown wooden postmortem case. He enters the kitchen and sees his colleague, Dr. John Slayter, already waiting to assist him. Dr. Slayter formally greets Dr. Allan, who acknowledges him in return and places his case on a chair near the table and the body. After removing his coat and washing his hands, Dr. Allan lifts the gold hasp on the case and looks inside, methodically reviewing the contents.

Firmly set in wooden blocks lined with purple velvet are two strong sectional knives with sharp, rounded belly blades and thick handles that reach to the palm. So, too, the case contains a standard scalpel, a probe pointed surgical knife, a thin-bladed knife (ten or twelve inches in length for cutting through internal organs), dissecting forceps, scissors, a stop-cork, a blow pipe, blunt ended probes of various lengths, a bone saw, a catheter, a mallet, a needle with strong thread, and a fine calibre compass.

Satisfied with the contents, Dr. Allan then surveys the room. The kitchen is well-lit with four windows. At Dr. Allan's request, Dr. Slayter opens one of the widows, allowing for a good flow of air. Dr. Allan then accounts for the other necessary items: a washbasin, buckets, hot and cold water, a bottle of watery solution, carbolic acid, some turpentine, and some carbolic linseed oil. So too, he counts clean rags, newspapers, three or four sponges, some soap, and a few towels. Periodically, throughout the autopsy, Dr. Allan and Dr. Slayter will dip and rub their hands in a bowl of cold water placed firmly between the legs of Alexander Allen.

Opening a notebook, Dr. Slayter keeps the record as Dr. Allan speaks.

Dr. Allan stares at the unwashed, still bloodied, face of Alexander Allen. "Approximate time of death," he says, "12:30 a.m., Thursday, September 8th. Approximate time since death and autopsy, eleven hours." Dr. Allen touches the body's arm. "The external temperature of the body," he adds, "cold to the touch." Dr. Allan puts his hands into the bowl between the body's legs, rubs them together, and then shakes off the cold water. With Dr. Slayter's assistance, he places a thick block beneath the body's shoulders, allowing the head to hang backward. Dr. Slayter takes up the notebook again.

"Name of the dead is Alexander Allen," Dr. Allan dictates. "He was, at the time of death approximately five and twenty years old." Dr. Allan now washes his hands in warm water and turpentine, then rinses again in the cold water. Pouring olive oil on his hands, which he rubs yet again, he then wipes his palms with a dry cloth. He wants to be sure, when the time comes, of having a solid grip on the autopsy instruments. He stands over the body and makes careful measurements of the shoulders and the circumference of the skull. "The dead man was a sailor, on Her Majesty's Ship, *Cumberland*," he says. "He is approximately five feet ten inches tall and of good proportion." He also notes that Allen appears in good physical health, save for the obvious injuries.

In my coffee shop, I take another sip from my cup. The blue sheep is still smiling. I am tempted to smile back but resist the urge. At another table, in the middle of the shop, a young man with a goatee sits alone. His left hand holds the handle of a plain white ceramic mug, a four-dollar cup of something with cinnamon-sprinkled-foam piled high. His right hand hovers over a sleek, black laptop computer. He stares at the screen while his right index finger slides over the touch sensitive mouse pad. Almost certainly, he is riding the obligatory wireless waves of all new-age coffee shops. Here, his customized e-ship can sail unfettered into any e-port around the world.

He smiles as he reads. Not the news from the Middle East, I am guessing.

In watching him, I am reminded of Henry David Thoreau, who coincidentally was finishing the final draft of his great work *Walden: or, Life in the Woods* at about the same time as Alexander Allen died. He said of such things technological, "Perhaps we are led oftener by the love of novelty, and a regard for the opinions of men, in procuring it, than by a true utility."

I smile at the thought. At least four people in this small coffee shop chat on cell phones. Five or so others sit with portable music plugged firmly into their ears. And, of course, just a few feet from me, my goateed e-surfer stares intently into his ethereal, otherworldly portal. Yes, the others in the coffee shop, perhaps five or six pairs of people, are actually talking to each other, but I am fairly confident that a cursory look in their purses or pockets would yield even more cell phones or iPods or MP3 players. Even in my small coffee shop, in my small city, on the far eastern coast of my adopted country, the denizens of the new Digital Age are quickly making obsolete the habits and values of a nearly two-century-old Industrial Age. But at what cost? Not surprisingly, Henry David Thoreau also recognized the dangers in a shift from old values and habits to new – but he happened to be observing the shift from the Agricultural Age to the Industrial Age.

The danger as he saw it was death by never having lived. He could not see the value in the technologies that were rapidly changing the world he knew. "Our inventions are wont to be pretty toys," he wrote, "which distract our attention from serious things. They are but improved means to an unimproved end, an end which it was already but too easy to arrive at; as railroads lead to Boston or New York. We are in great haste to construct a magnetic telegraph from Maine to Texas; but Maine and Texas, it may be, have nothing important to communicate."

As I look around my misplaced Mediterranean coffee shop, watching my goateed friend sail to some faraway e-port for 'information' and watching the others in the café talk with disembodied voices and listen to disembodied singers, I consider that perhaps our collective attention was being distracted from serious things, from what was happening in the here and now.

How did the Buddhists describe it? Mindfulness?

Then again, perhaps there is no 'here' anymore. And without a 'here,' there is no 'now.' And without a 'now,' there is no 'then,' and of course, there can be no 'will be.' In other words, there is no responsibility or obligation to a past or a future, no sense of place or purpose, just an endless pursuit of distracting, empty noise and empty pleasure to while away the time. This death of context means no true existence – just postmodern digital death.

Maybe Thoreau was right.

Then again, maybe I just needed more coffee.

So I take another sip and think for a moment more about Henry David Thoreau as he prepared to publish *Walden* in 1854. "I went to the woods," wrote Thoreau, "because I wished to live deliberately, to front only the essential facts of life, and see if I could not learn what it had to teach, and not, when I came to die, discover that I had not lived." In thinking about death – digital and otherwise – I am transported back to the autopsy room in the Poorhouse just a few dozen yards away.

"The cut on the right side of Allen's forehead was parallel with, and just above, the eyebrow, about an inch in length," says Dr. Allan, gently touching the wound. "It is not a serious cut. Over the left eye, however, is a gash at a forty-five degree angle, of an inch and a half, likely the result of a sharp instrument." In the centre of the forehead, Dr. Allan detects a small bruise with some grains of sand on it. Intrigued, he returns to the other cuts but finds no grains. Dr. Allan then notes that the face has a scratch or two more, but nothing else.

He moves away from the head, down to the torso. He sees nothing and moves further down, to the groin. There, Dr. Allan finds an oval bruise on the right side, four inches long and two inches wide. He looks up at Dr. Slayter, who also acknowledges the bruise. "A kick would have done it," says Dr. Allan. Dr. Slayter nods, and makes the appropriate notation. Then Dr. Allan moves down along the legs. He finds two or three scratches on the knees.

The examination of the body complete, Dr. Allan walks around to the head. On the way, he takes a scalpel from the postmortem box. With it firmly in hand, he plants his feet, then cuts and removes Alexander Allen's scalp. Dr. Allan notes that the hair is thick, curly, and black. On the exposed skull, he slides his finger along a fracture that starts at the base and moves to the top. He looks up at Dr. Slayter. "This was the cause of death," he says, "some heavy blow that fractured the skull to cause a massive trauma." He would later say, "It was the greatest fracture ever came under my notice." Dr. Allan would also later concede that a fall from a window, twenty-two feet up, might have caused the injuries he catalogued – but that it was unlikely. "Certainly," Dr. Allan said, "a man just dropping to the ground from the window could not have sustained such a fracture."

He then finds a deep contusion on the skull the size of a silver dollar. He indicates that it could have been received from a fall depending on what the head struck. Dr. Allan knows that a blow to the head often produces a fracture on the opposite side, and so, if the man had fallen from the window as described, the fracture should be on the top. Given the fracture he had noted, the blow must have occurred over the ear. This fracture ran in a straight line. Dr. Allan tells Dr. Slayter that he once read where the Duke of Orleans had fallen from his horse and died of a fracture similar to this.

Dr. Allan again looks at the wound over the right eye. He is certain that the cut came from a sharp object. "The arteries about the temples are rich and a wound in that area produces much blood," Dr. Allan says, "so long as the heart continues to beat." He looks at Dr. Slayter. "Had he lived for even five minutes after the blows to his forehead," he says, "there would have been much blood."

Dr. Slayter points to the left side of the head.

"Yes," says Dr. Allan, "the hair on the left side of the head is clotted with blood, but given the lack of blood in that area of the body, the wounds over the eyes must have come earlier in the evening. There was too little blood on the clothes, provided he lived for enough time after the wounds to the eyes. Those wounds to the eyes must have been followed by the blow to the head that killed him."

Dr. Allan then takes a seat. He and Dr. Slayter consider the fall from the window.

"He would have been stunned," says Dr. Slayter, closing the notebook and placing it on a small table. "I have not the least doubt that the fracture on the skull was caused by a blow at the point of depression by some instrument. There was no incision." Dr. Slayter points at the head. "No man could have received such a blow and walked afterwards. He must have been stunned. Such a blow must have produced immediate death. In one of the wounds over the eye, you noted that, on raising the integument, the indentation in the skull was found to be of the same length as the cut in the flesh. The only reasonable conclusion is that it was inflicted with a sharp instrument – and with force. I do not think it possible for a man who fell twenty feet and received such a fracture to have moved many feet. As well, I do not think such a fracture could have taken place by a fall on the feet." Dr. Allan nods and looks again at the body. Dr. Slayter continues his thought: "He might have fallen on his feet and pitched forward. But no fall could have produced the two cuts and the fracture."

Dr. Allan agrees. Someone who fell from a window at that distance, and received such a blow to the head, would not have moved far before dying. Dr. Allan and Dr. Slayter then stand and walk to the postmortem box. Dr. Allan reaches for another scalpel, and positions himself by the torso of the body. In a firm, deliberate motion, he cuts open the stomach. With a probe given to him by Dr. Slayter, he examines the innards. He looks carefully for evidence that Alexander Allen might have been drinking alcohol that night, but he detects nothing. From this examination, and having smelled the body's mouth earlier at the Police Office, Dr. Allan tells Dr. Slayter he is certain that little or no alcohol had been consumed.

With that, the autopsy is complete. Both Dr. Allan and Dr. Slayter wash their hands in warm water, soap, and turpentine. The autopsy tools are also washed and carefully placed back in their velvet-lined wooden case. Dr. Allan and Dr. Slayter cover the body, close the window, put on their coats, and then leave the Poorhouse. Dr. Allan returns home to rest and to review his notes. Then on Friday, September 9, he testifies at the Coroner's Inquest.

On that Friday morning, before the Inquest begins, city clerk James Clarke returns to the Waterloo. He carefully notes the distance from the sill of Myers' window to the ground: twenty-two feet. He sees that the body was found some nine feet away. "Inside," he recalls, "I could perceive no marks of blood on any portion of the premises and nothing whatever to indicate the commission of a murder. The floors did not appear to have been scrubbed. I did perceive some drops of blood on the doorway of the taproom that were evidently of no recent date."

Upstairs, in Myers' room, Clarke makes careful measurements. "From the bottom of the floor to the sill of the window is two feet seven and a half inches," he recalls, "the lower sash, two feet two inches, and the width of the sash three feet three inches. The lower sash had two panes of glass in it. I think it was eight by ten glass. Looking out that window, it did occur to me that a man might hold on by his hands and drop to the steps. Of course, the steps were very high, steep and narrow."

Clarke takes one last look around the room and then walks out into the hall and down the stairs. In the stairwell, a window looks to the south. "If something had happened in the room," reasons Clarke looking from the window down the narrow stairwell, "then Allen would have been brought down these stairs. So I examined the banisters leading from the landing to the entry." He grabs the banister. "The lower one is very weak. No struggle could take place without breaking. If I shoved my back against it, it would break." Still, there is no blood upstairs, on the entry landing walls or windowsill. "The south stop was out," he observes, "but in many houses, these stops are very lightly put in." With his examination finished, Clarke leaves the Waterloo and heads to the inquest at the courthouse.

Later, Dr. Allan also revisits the Waterloo with the Inquest jury. There, he remarks that "a man jumping out of that window in question could not have sustained those injuries, viewing the ground, etc., could not have obtained this fracture on the skull. I observed the stop out of the window and thought it very strange that any man could jump out of the window with the sash out. If a person sprung out of the window he would have fell outside of the steps."

Throughout the day that Friday, six sailors and six civilians sit at the Coroner's Inquest and listen to the assembled testimony and evidence. They hear from local citizens and visiting sailors, from witnesses at the Waterloo and the watchmen, from James Clarke and Dr. Allan. Though the investigation produces little in the way of concrete evidence, enough inconsistencies exist to suggest that this was not an accident.

In my coffee shop, I put down my notebook and finish my coffee. My blue sheep remains insistently smiling, but I do not. In his Friday morning tour through the Waterloo, James Clarke unearthed enough evidence to hint that something darker had happened that night at the tavern. So too, the inquest also found enough evidence for them to believe that murder had likely been committed. The judgment resulted in John Gordon, Thomas Murphy, Matilda Ballard, Mary Anne Cole, Sarah Myers and David Parsons all being charged with the crime.

I read again part of Dr. Allan's statement at the Inquest. "Neither of the blows to the brow could produce the fracture," he had said. "The fracture extends from the top of the scull down the left side, behind the ear and ends at the lower part of the scull. There was a depression above the ear, which would have been sufficient to produce the fracture."

This, of course, had been noted before.

But then Dr. Allan adds this: "Fractures can occur where death does not take place until after considerable bleeding occurs in the brain. It is therefore possible for death to be both immediate and also delayed. Therefore, it is also possible that an earlier blow to the head, like that above the eye, could start fluid buildup which could later trigger death, even from a non-fatal blow, like that above the eye."

This single comment from Dr. Allan makes the testimony of Alexander Allen's fellow sailors compelling. They describe the events that occurred earlier in the evening of September 7, before Alexander Allen arrived at the Waterloo. According to them, Alexander Allen received another injury that night – another blow to the head. I decide to unearth what I can about that last day of Alexander Allen's life.

But first, I needed to better understand the life of a sailor in the Age of Sail.

Chapter 7

The Sailor

In 1805, after years of meticulously measuring and carefully calculating the billowing of sails, a young British seaman named Francis Beaufort humbly presented to His Majesty's Royal Navy a universal scale of his own creation, one that measured – in neatly defined categories of 0 to 12 – the force of wind on sails at sea. The British Navy, true to its reputation as an efficient and forward-looking institution, rightly recognized in Beaufort's submission an invaluable contribution to the glory of British natural science and the cause of British maritime supremacy – then promptly filed and forgot it.

Meantime, while waiting for the Royal Navy's response to his submission, the young Francis Beaufort began meticulously measuring and carefully calculating all sorts of similarly fascinating stuff, until one day, some thirty years later, in 1838 – at the dawn of the Victorian era and the Golden Age of Sail – someone deep in the military bureaucracy said aloud what a good idea it would be if the Royal Navy could measure the force of wind on sails at sea. As it turns out, someone in the room vaguely remembered that another person had once asked that same question, and that he had even tried to answer it.

So after some confused searching through the basement files, the Beaufort Wind Scale was duly rediscovered, dusted off, and officially deemed the Wind Scale of Her Majesty's Royal Navy. The scale was soon so popular, in fact, that the Royal Navy awarded the now not-so-young Francis Beaufort a full admiralship, for which Beaufort kindly thanked everyone at the Royal Navy office, and then promptly began meticulously researching and carefully measuring whatever it was that struck his fancy at the time.

At least that's how I remember the story on a Saturday morning in early autumn as I walk determinedly east into a steady rain blowing determinedly west. Blowing rain comes so often to this city by the sea that few if any locals are much discouraged from venturing out into a blustery rain for the silliest of reasons. That said, my journey today is serious: I am searching for "Jack Tar" in the Golden Age of Sail.

For the last six or eight weeks, when time allowed, I pursued the myriad details of the mariner's life in and out of local libraries and provincial archives. I read old books and new articles, perused painted pictures and fading photographs. But after one too many dry descriptions of "life at sea" – and one too many unintended naps in the public library's comfortable seating – I abandoned my amateur scholarly work for a more tangible approach, a grittier, gut-felt examination of "the sailor's life." I needed the smell of sea salt in my nostrils and the rush of wind against my face.

Admittedly, though, I didn't need the rain.

Still, with my cherry red raincoat zipped to the chin and my hood pulled low on my head, I venture out on my quest again with much enthusiasm, my notebook and pen at the ready. My destination is east, to the waterfront, in search of the longstanding keeper of Halifax's tangible maritime past – the Maritime Museum of the Atlantic.

With the rain steadily falling, I walk across the Commons, then south for a block along Brunswick Street. I turn left, down three blocks to Barrington Street, and then right a few blocks further south to Sackville Street. At the corner of Barrington and Sackville, I face a rough mugging of sideways wind and stinging rain that knocks me off balance and snaps my hood off my head. Awkwardly, I regain my footing and reapply my hood. Then I tuck my chin down to my chest and lean forward into the wind, walking slowly east to the bottom of Sackville Street, where – checking for cars in either direction, and seeing none – I dash across Lower Water Street into a large courtyard of geometrically arranged cement and stone.

There, I am greeted by a large bronze statue standing on a squared pedestal of granite. The pedestal is faced with four polished, bronze panels screwed into the stone. The panels depict relief outlines of ships. Beneath these is an inscription. It tells me that the bronze sailor above – twice the size of an average man – was caste to commemorate the sailors who left from Halifax to fight in World War I and World War II.

I look at the statue.

Certainly, the sculpture nicely captures the popular image of sailors in the early and mid-twentieth century. Yet the clothes – the open, long-collared shirt; the wide, bell-bottomed pants; and the rimless, round cap – all hint at sailors from a hundred years earlier, perhaps even hint at all sailors who, for 250 years, have left the shores of Halifax Harbour, heading out to sea. This sailor is animated in frozen half stride – chest out, chin up – walking briskly toward the harbour, toward some unseen, waiting ship. Over his right shoulder rests a long pack, rolled tight and tied in four places. In his left hand hangs a cylindrical duffel bag with rope tied at the top. Though the sailor walks toward the water, he also, at the same moment, turns his head back toward the shore, toward someone, perhaps, saying goodbye.

Shore relationships for sailors were then, as likely they are now, tenuous, complicated affairs, often enough emotionally straining. Historian Margaret Creighton, in her essay "American Mariners and the Rites of Manhood, 1830-1870," looks at songs sung in the Golden Age of Sail that speak to relationships. I have recorded two sets of lyrics in my notebook.

One reads:

> A sailor loves a gallant ship
> And messmates bold and free
> And even welcomes with delight
> Saturday night at sea

> One hour each week we'll snatch from care
> As through the world we roam
> And think of dear ones far away
> And all the joys from home

The other goes like this:

> How happy is a sailor's life
> From coast to coast to roam
> In every port to find a wife
> In every land a home

The first song, an introspective lament for home and hearth, is juxtaposed against a rowdy song of unattached masculinity. And yet, on reflection, Creighton argues that both might well be ironic, speaking to something deeper, something more complicated in the relationships among sailors and their families, among sailors and prostitutes.

Creighton argues that many married sailors were haunted by thoughts of infidelity. In this context, the two songs suggest a different type of lament and boast. The first song idealizes home rather than admits the fear born of physical and emotional distance and distrust. It is noteworthy that the reality of life on land often drove sailors back to sea, to a life and rhythm they better understood. The second song, in this context, speaks to the sailor's efforts to fill the emotional void caused by life at sea. It speaks to the peculiar, sometime habit of buying temporary 'marriages' in each port of call. That is, sailors would pay for a prostitute's fidelity during the time they were in port. In this sense, the second song is a sad wish for the stable, familial intimacy denied to sailors of the day.

Life as a sailor came with distinct rituals, rights, and rules at sea all existing in isolation from – and often in counterpoint to – those on land. Despite romantic tales, little romance existed in the sailor's life. In more cases than not, young men went to sea to escape a grinding poverty and difficult lives in the towns and villages of New Brunswick and Nova Scotia. But the escape was only partial. The conditions aboard ship were often brutal – poor food and dangerous work. No doubt, these hardships wove deep bonds among sailors, bonds that were perhaps deeper than those tenuous connections with family back home.

I stare intently at the youthful, rain-soaked face of the bronze sailor. The raindrops moving down the cheeks give the face a subtle suggestion of life. I wonder, "Is this is the face of Jack Tar?"

Jack Tar was the generic, oft-used common name given to seamen in the late nineteenth century. The origins of the nickname are obscure, but some maritime historians suggest it was born of the waterproof tarpaulin coats and hats the sailors wore. Others suggest that the name originated with the pigtails the sailors commonly had, which they often smeared with tar to keep them from getting tangled in the rigging. And still others say that the nickname came from sailors who constantly heaved at the tar-soaked rigging, staining their hands black. Whatever the source, the name Jack Tar stuck.

What did a typical Jack Tar look like? My dry reading tells me that his average age in the early nineteenth century was twenty-six. He was just over five and a half feet tall, oval-faced, and muscular. Compared to modern, well-fed males, Jack Tar was thinner and more sinewy. Likely, he wore a tattoo, a name or initials inside a rounded heart, or anchors proudly proclaiming his profession on the back of his hands. His clothing, even in the British Navy, varied greatly. No standard uniform was introduced until 1857. Until then, sailors purchased clothes from a "slop" chest onboard ship. Still, even after uniform regulations were introduced, seamen created their own clothes from government supplied cloth. Only in the twentieth century did the British Navy provide ready-made uniforms. Because of its slow evolution at the hands of the sailors, the elements of sailors' clothes reflected the practical needs of the sailors' life. The familiar long collar, notable on the bronze statue, was created to keep clean the seaman's jacket when sailors kept their pigtails long. Some sailors wore tarred jackets and wide-kneed trousers and striped or checked shirts. The open-collar shirt and white bell-bottomed pants were for comfort and ease of movement. The brimless hat was preferred because it stayed on in windy weather and while working high in the rigging.

This was Jack Tar.

Alexander Allen, the dead sailor, lying on a makeshift autopsy table in the kitchen of the Poorhouse was a Jack Tar, too. From the fragmentary evidence, we know he was born in 1828 or 1829 in a hamlet called Caithness located on the southwest corner of New Brunswick, on the small Passmaquoddy Bay leading south into the Bay of Fundy. Like so many of his generation, he grew up in the poverty of village life where he might have become a fisherman or farmer. Instead, in a story familiar to New Brunswick and Nova Scotia, he was drawn to the promise and adventure of the sea. On the eve of his death, he was twenty-four or twenty-five and had reached the rank of Able Seaman on the third-rate H.M.S. *Cumberland*. He was described as "very prepossessing in appearance" with dark curly hair and a strong physique. The surgeon of the H.M.S. *Cumberland*, Thomas Fraser, noted that Alexander Allen had "never been on the sick list." On September 7, 1853, he came ashore a hundred or so yards north along the waterfront from where I stand, as animated as this bronze statue suggests.

The face of this bronze Jack Tar mixes gently in my mind with the image of Alexander Allen, as each walks on shore, frozen in mid-stride. I imagine the face of the bronze Jack Tar as Alexander Allen's face, young, with blue-grey eyes that have seen something of the world in its day – the exotic foreign ports, the storms at sea, the bottles of West Indian rum, and the stunning view of an equatorial sunset on the horizon. With Alexander Allen's face etched in my mind, I turn away from the bronze statue and walk a block north along Lower Water Street, to the Maritime Museum of the Atlantic.

The museum is housed in a boxy, two-floor modern building juxtaposed against an old brick and stone warehouse. The warehouse is a former hardware store, owned and operated by four generations, which closed in the 1970s. As I reach the museum entrance, I read a white and black rent-a-sign on the sidewalk. A plaintive barker's encouragement is pasted on the white surface: "Come and See the Lego Train Exhibit." The cheapness of the sign and the directness of the message leave me feeling a bit morose. In a digital age of interactive computer play-stations and widescreen plasma screens, the Maritime Museum desperately competes for the attention of the young.

Given the museum's likely chances in the competition, I'm left wondering about its future – just a sailing ship's chance in an age of steam, I suppose.

Inside the museum's vestibule, I shake the rain from my coat and fold it over my arm. Then I walk to the Visitor's Desk, where a young woman wearing a white knit sweater, brown corduroy pants, and a rectangular plastic nametag – Alyson – waits patiently to greet me. She smiles.

"A pass for one?" she asks.

For a moment I look to the right of Alyson into the open museum. It's relatively quiet. I see two dozen people or so – parents and children – gathered together in congenial family groups, looking at this and that. I feel oddly out of place as I look back to Alyson. She is still smiling, still waiting patiently for my answer. I can't help wondering, in this family museum setting, how many single museum passes are sold – particularly to someone clearly having walked some distance in a steady, blowing rain. None, I'm guessing.

I smile back at Alyson. "Yes, " I say, "just one."

She pulls together the requisite floor maps and promotional flyers, while I pick up my pink plastic museum pin. I mention that I'm looking for the exhibit on the Age of Sail. She smiles again and pertly points to the stairwell behind me. In one breath, she relates a convoluted set of directions. "Go to those stairs," she says, "just over there, to your left, where you head to the top of the stairwell, and take a left when you get to the top, turning right through the doorway, not the left doorway mind you, the right, and then turn left again, and head down a short hall, where you'll find you are right in the Days of Sail exhibit." I'm still staring at Alyson waiting for her to breathe, when I realize she's finished her directions. Admittedly, I've already forgotten them and am concerned she might pass out due to oxygen deprivation if I ask her to repeat it all. So I just thank her and clip on my pink museum pin. I'll explore the main floor of the museum first.

The collection on the first floor is, to say the least, eclectic. To my right, a live parrot climbs the outside of a metal cage. He seems decidedly uninterested in the adults trying to elicit a response by endlessly saying "hello" in what they apparently assume is a parrot dialect. Across from the parrot, the set of a children's television program lays spread out behind glass. The set shows Halifax Harbour in miniature, populated by tugboats, bridges, and buildings. Strangely, each of the inanimate objects has eyes. Just around a corner, a collection of small sailboats and a birchbark canoe rest on wooden bases, the canoe behind glass. Around another corner still, a temporary cut and paste, bristle-board display tells the story of Irish immigration to Saint John, New Brunswick. At the back wall of the main floor, a large plate-glass window faces out on to the harbour. I walk to the glass and for a few minutes watch an enormous container ship, piled impossibly high with large metal boxes, glide silently through the water, heading slowly out to sea. When it passes, I return to the displays, walking back through the Irish Immigration exhibit and around a darkened corner. There, I stumble onto the museum's permanent exhibit of the Halifax Explosion, the largest man-made explosion prior to the atomic bomb. Of all the ghosts that haunt this city, the Halifax Explosion may haunt it the loudest.

Caused by the collision of two war ships, the French ship *Mont Blanc* and the Norwegian ship *Imo*, the Halifax Explosion devastated the city. At 7:30 in the morning on December 6, 1917, the *Mont Blanc* moved through the tight harbour Narrows laden with 2,300 tons of picric acid and some 200 tons of TNT all destined for the war in Europe. The *Imo* moved through the Narrows as well, in the other direction. The two ships collided, and a fire started on the *Mont Blanc*. For twenty minutes, the fire burned as the terrified crew abandoned ship and rowed for the Dartmouth shore. Meantime, people onshore watched the strange spectacle in the harbour. The *Mont Blanc* finally exploded at 9:05 in the morning – a time eerily captured on a museum pocket-watch, frozen at the moment of impact. It was said of the explosion that the water in the Narrows was momentarily displaced, revealing the harbour bottom – a truly biblical description of an apocalyptic explosion. Huge fragments of the *Mont Blanc* sailed five and a half kilometres away. I reach down and touch two of these fragments, resting on a painted wooden frame – large, unrecognizable twisted chunks of metal.

The display cases tell me that 1,630 homes in the north end of the Halifax shore were levelled by the impact. Another 12,000 homes were terribly damaged. The human costs were even more horrifying. Nearly 2,000 people – men, women, and children – were killed and thousands more were injured. Among those living, 6,000 were left homeless to face an impending winter storm. The museum skillfully brings the enormity of the disaster down to human scale. In a glass case to my left rests a light blue baby's dress with an open white collar. It isn't until I am standing over the dress that I realize it is flecked with dark brown spots, and still a moment more before I realize that the spots are nearly hundred-year-old bloodstains. With a surprising gut-wrenching suddenness, the explosion is very personal. In another glass case, other personal effects – watches, books, cutlery, and more – all sit frozen in time, as though dropped at the moment of impact.

Then, as quickly as I came upon it, the Halifax Explosion exhibit ends, and I pass through a small exhibit of World War II with displays of water mines and torpedoes. At the end of that exhibit, I make my way to the west staircase and up to the second floor. There, I am greeted by another of Halifax's loud ghosts – the *Titanic*.

When the *Titanic* sank in 1912, Halifax received many of her survivors – and many of her dead, buried in three city cemeteries. In glass cases, the museum has displayed the *Titanic*'s scant flotsam, twenty artifacts that include a curiously well-preserved wooden deck chair unfolded behind a large pane of glass. Near to it, in an interactive space, a replica of the chair has been built and set on a replica segment of the *Titanic*'s deck. As I come upon it, a bored, teenaged boy sits in the chair, idly thumbing a cell phone. Next to him, also behind glass, sits a carved, wooden newel post face from one of the *Titanic*'s Grand Staircase landings. The piece is placed next to a striking seven foot by seven foot black and white photograph of the Grand Staircase. The effect is spectacular, providing a stunning hint of the ship's grandeur. The *Titanic* exhibit ends with a small, glass, cylindrical container holding a rusticle, which was removed from the *Titanic* as she sat on the bottom of the cold Atlantic. The rusticle is similar to an icicle and forms underwater on metal shipwrecks. As the display explains, the rusticle is alive – sort of. About a third of it is iron oxide and two-thirds is microbes, bacteria, and fungi that use the ship's metal as food. This process of metal consumption creates corrosion as a waste product, thus forming the rusticle. I muse that the *Titanic* may well be alive in more than just popular memory.

In the next section, adjacent to the *Titanic* exhibit, the museum has displayed a series of older shipwrecks – the stories and the artifacts. One wreck in particular catches my attention: the American steamer *Humbolt*, which sank on December 5, 1853, just a few months after the death of Alexander Allen. The ship ran aground at Chebucto Head and then made its way to Portuguese Cove before sinking. All aboard, according to the description provided, survived. My eye is drawn to two gold pocket watches in the *Humbolt*'s display case, both missing the hands and covers. The roman numerals on the faces are still clear. For a moment, in my mind's eye, I imagine one of these watches, restored, in the hands of the sailor, Alexander Allen.

A few yards from the *Humbolt*'s armless watches a painting hangs of the *America*, which steamed into Halifax Harbour on February 14, 1859. In the painting, the harbour is uncharacteristically frozen. As described below the painting, the arrival of the steamer created a stir as the ship smashed through the ice. The painter, using some artistic license, places the citizens of the day skating on the frozen harbour not far from the *America* as it cuts through the ice. Beneath the painting, adding to the effect, the museum has placed two wooden skates with loose leather straps. Each skate has a rusted metal blade that curls in winding loops at the toes.

I walk away from the painting and the skates, turn a corner, and enter the museum's single largest display – the Age of Steam exhibit. Along one long wall, rows and rows of shelves jut themselves out into the hall, overwhelming the visitor with nautical 'stuff.' Hundreds of wooden and metal objects from steamships line the glass shelves in no particular order that I can discern. Out on the floor, encased in rectangular boxes of glass, models of steamers sit in historical stasis. In looking at them, I am struck by the extraordinary ugliness of the vessels – the harsh lines of smokestacks and, on the early ships, the metalworks of the water wheels. In one case sits a one-foot model of Samuel Cunard's first steamship, the *Britannia*. It is the ship – or at least the model of the ship – that brought Charles Dickens to Halifax.

Standing by the wee-*Britannia*, a shaven-headed, pierced-lipped, iPod-wearing young girl gives the model a five-second look. She yawns, then wanders off to another display. Sharing her opinion, I also leave the *Britannia* and survey the other cases of steamships through the twentieth century. Try as I do to like them, the industrial age ugliness of the Age of Steam display discourages me. So I wander back through the Age of Steam exhibit in an effort to find the Age of Sail display, but I can't manage to get my bearings.

Lost in the *Titanic* section again, I sit in the now empty reproduction deck chair on the faux-deck. From my pocket, I remove a piece of paper, unfold it, and look at it. It is the Robert Wilkie painting of Halifax Harbour from the Dartmouth shore. I look again at the Red Mill windmill, at trees and the fields in the foreground, and at the smoke rising from distant stacks on the Halifax side. But this time, I pay particular attention to the water, or more accurately, to the ships anchored in the water.

I focus on one large ship with three masts. A description reads, "The large vessel is probably the H.M.S. *Cumberland* …" This is the ship on which Alexander Allen sailed. This coincidence resonates further as I read on: "A very similar engraved 'View of Halifax, Nova Scotia from the Red Mill, Dartmouth' appeared in Gleason's Pictorial Drawing-Room Companion, Boston Mass., 10 September 1853." It is the date – 10 September 1853 – that strikes me: just three days after the death of Alexander Allen, and the same date of the newspaper clipping reporting Alexander Allen's death.

In an age when photographs were rare, and outdoor photographs even more so, this painting of the Halifax Harbour, and of the H.M.S. *Cumberland*, provides me with the closest thing I can find to a snapshot of the time and place of the death. So I take one last look at the details of the ship as it sits in the placid water under a near cloudless sky. Then I fold the paper, place it back in my pocket, and wander off to find the Days of Sail exhibit.

The task still proves challenging, however, as I twice find myself back at the *Titanic* exhibit. Finally, accepting my apparent natural sense of directionlessness, I consult my museum map and manage to locate a doorway leading into a brightly lit hallway. Halfway down the hallway, I see a small sign that reads Days of Sail with an even smaller arrow pointing left. So I follow the arrow, turning left, then right, finally arriving, by the grace of fate, at the door of the exhibit.

Like the Age of Sail in history, this exhibit space is tucked away, far from the other exhibits, almost forgotten by time. The room is empty as I enter it — eerily so, in fact. Immediately, my senses other than sight take over: I smell the wood, the rope, and the tar; I hear the floorboards creaking beneath my feet and hear waves rolling and crashing on unseen speakers. The wooden walls are filled with pictures and dioramas of ships with billowing sails. On the floor sit coils of thick rope, some four feet high. More rope winds itself along the floor and walls. On wooden pillars in the middle of the room are affixed figureheads of painted, buxom women. The whole collection of sight and sound gives one the feeling of stepping out of time and place, into a world at once slower and more attuned to the elements.

In glass rectangular cases in the centre of the room, model ships sit frozen in snapshot waves. By contrast to the Age of Steam ships, I am struck by the elegance of the sailing ships. Perhaps it is the warmth of wood or the balanced geometry of the spider web rigging. Or perhaps I am just drawn to the ships' absolute dependence on nature for movement, on the winds and on the tide. After walking about the room, I sit on a coil of rope, again remove the folded paper from my pocket, and look at the H.M.S. *Cumberland*.

At 2,214 tons, she was a grand vessel, carrying between 500 to 720 men, and boasting nearly seventy guns. She was the sixth British ship named *Cumberland*, a third-rate ship, launched 21 October 1842. The designation third-rate meant that she was a ship of the line with sixty-four to eighty guns on two decks. She was also the flagship of Vice-Admiral George Francis Seymour, commanded by Captain George Henry Seymour and regularly sailed the waters between Halifax and the West Indies. That said, she would, after leaving behind the body of Alexander Allen in 1853, head back to Europe and eventually to the conflict in the Crimea. And so, for awhile, I look at the picture of the *Cumberland*. Then I walk about the room, admiring the displays.

As I move, I think about the other exhibits I've seen today, about the bronze Jack Tar outside, about sailors and their life. I steep myself in all these images and words. Alexander Allen was becoming more tangible to me now – and his death somehow more personal, more tragic. Sure, these sailors faced many perils, and Allen could have died in a number of tragic ways. Storms, for instance, frequently occurred at sea, but in truth these ships were well-designed to withstand the vagaries of the weather. That said, such ships could easily be punished by wind, driven into rocks or to shore.

In my notebook, I have recorded the harrowing description of a close call by a seventeenth-century English sailor named Edward Coxere. "We suddenly saw the land on the weather bow," he wrote, "a sad sight with the sea raging on the rocks at one side and it falling so violently on us on the other side, which was such a dismal sight to us as is hard to be expressed the manner of it, so violently did the sea press us towards the shore, insomuch that we were forced to let run our yards and sails down and cut away our mainmast and hove yards and sails overboard and put overboard one anchor. We finding the sea heaving us still to the shore, we put over another anchor and, finding the wind and sea still press us to the shore and but little more drift, we cut overboard our foremast and put over another anchor, which was the last we had to trust to."

Sailors of the age faced other challenges that could easily result in death, challenges that historian David James Stewart explores in his dissertation, *Rocks and Storms I'll Fear No More*. Illness, accident, and war were all great dangers to sailors. Illness, says Stewart, was a constant threat. By some accounts, disease was responsible for half the Royal Navy deaths during the Napoleonic Wars. On board, scurvy and beriberi – illnesses caused by vitamin deficiencies C and B respectively – were potent killers. So too was typhus. Poorly maintained ships were thick with filth. Typhus found agreeable breeding grounds among unwashed sailors on unwashed ships. In fact, hammocks – the swaying beds of sailors – were introduced to keep sailors from sleeping on the decks where typhus would breed. As well, the regular task of swabbing the deck each morning was demanded, in part, to control disease. Of course, many diseases were not contracted on boats. On shore, sailors could easily acquire venereal diseases, yellow fever, and more.

Accidents, says Stewart, were also a common cause of death, drowning in particular. Few sailors were encouraged to learn how to swim for fear they would desert. As such, being swept off a deck by a cresting wave would often as not prove fatal. Similarly, working in the complicated rigging found sailors falling to their deaths on the deck or in the water. The same Richard Henry Dana, Jr. who once described Halifax's Barrack Street was aboard an American brig in 1834 and witnessed the death of one sailor. "A sailor was going aloft," he wrote, "to fit a strap round the main top-mast-head, for ringtail halyards, and had the strap and block, a coil of halyards, and a marline-spike about his neck. He fell from the starboard futtock shrouds, and not knowing how to swim, and being heavily dressed, with all those things round his neck, he probably sank immediately."

And, according to Stewart, a surprisingly small percentage of sailors were killed in battle. By one estimate, only about six percent of British sailors engaged in combat were killed in the Napoleonic Wars.

Sitting in the Days of Sail room, thinking of the many ways that a sailor might die, I muse that fewer still were killed by "supposed murder." I decide it is time to leave, and so I exit the Days of Sail room. I find a stairwell to the main floor and head out of the museum, back out into a light rain. I walk around the building to the waterfront and stand on one of the many wharves. There, I am buffeted by the relentless wind. The gusts again remind me of the Beaufort Wind Scale, which, despite being a product of the nineteenth century, is still in use today – with some notable modifications. No longer does the scale look solely at the wind, but also at the sea. So too – in a distressing sign of the times, I suppose – the scale now climbs past the top number, twelve, to a robust seventeen, accommodating the growing ferocity of hurricanes in a modern age of runaway carbon emissions and climate change.

With the blowing rain pattering against my raincoat, I look at the rolling harbour water, and I recall what I can about the Beaufort measurements. At 0 on the scale, sea conditions are flat, while smoke from chimneys rises straight into the air. At 3, a gentle breeze folds large wavelets with breaking crests and scattered whitecaps, while the leaves and smaller twigs of trees wave in constant motion. At 6, a strong breeze whips up large waves with cresting foam and spraying water, while tree branches sway. At 9, a strong gale churns up three-metre waves with thick foam and heavy spray, while on land, small structures reluctantly give up bits of themselves to the lashing wind. At 12, hurricane force winds raise huge fourteen-metre waves replete with foam and spray that obscures the ocean water, while on land, good-sized buildings simply call it quits.

Admittedly, I like the subjective quality of the scale – more a poetic read of wind and water than an accurate, measurable science. In a real sense, the Beaufort Scale nicely fits the Golden Age of Sail into which it was born, a marriage of the Age of Reason with the Age of Romance. In the spirit of that age long passed, I playfully measure the gruff howl of wind and the undulating roll of the water and gauge the day's gale at 3.

With the day winding down, and having learned what I can about sailors and the sea, I head home. Along the way, I think of Alexander Allen and the city in September of 1853. I consider that the age – the time and place – is still vaguely connected to the present through the sea and the structures. But as the Age of Sail gave way to the Age of Steam, so too the Industrial Age now gives way to the Digital Age. And with that passing comes the risk of snapping our tenuous connections to the past and the birth of a willful amnesia encouraged by an age infatuated with fleeting emotive moments in wide-screen mediums. I wonder: does the demise of the Maritime Museum of the Atlantic suggest the demise of the stories that shape us? Does it mean the disappearance of our ghosts? I don't have a ready answer, not in a steady rain with a growing dampness creeping into my shirt, at any rate.

I am uncertain about where my mystery will lead, but feel more strongly than ever that I should follow the ghosts – wherever they lead. After all, it's one thing to lose the present to the past, but quite another to lose the past altogether.

With that in mind, I prepare to follow Alexander Allen through his last day.

Chapter 8

The Fight

In nineteenth-century music, the theory of bitonality held that two distinct musical keys could exist at the same moment within a single piece of music. Russian composer Igor Stravinsky famously explored this theory in his 1911 ballet, *Petrushka*, in which one clarinet plays a melody in the key of C major, while another clarinet riffs on the same melody – but in the key of F sharp. The resulting music was jarring to the ears, but it somehow worked, perhaps reflecting the jarring nature of the early twentieth century.

I find myself thinking about bitonality one morning, while sitting on a cold cement stair, drinking a black coffee from a paper cup, and looking out over a slow-moving crowd in the downtown Halifax Farmers' Market. Each Saturday morning, hundreds of people come to this Farmers' Market to buy their vegetables and talk with their neighbours, collectively sharing a vibrant rhythm of life unbroken in this city for more than 250 years.

Watching the movement of people, I muse that bitonality was likely born of Industrial Age dissonance, the groaning and squealing of factory machines, and the huffing and coughing of steam engines. Naturally enough, the serious composers of the period were listening.

And as steam engines gave way to gas engines, and the huffing and coughing gave way to growling and roaring, more serious musicians pushed beyond the theory of bitonality into the chaotic, polyphonic, mushroom-cloud discordance of atonality, which dismissed altogether keys and tonalities. If nothing else, this explains Ornette Coleman and the Sex Pistols.

This weekly Farmers' Market is the direct descendant of the 1850s curbside Cheapside Market, which itself is a direct descendant of the first Halifax farmers' market established in June of 1750. But unlike those markets, this farmers' market resides inside, along a labyrinth of arched stone passageways in the old Alexander Keith's Brewery complex, a collection of three or four brick and stone buildings constructed between 1822 and 1863. The arched stone passageways lead to a series of courtyards that were once opened to the air but are now covered by steel roofs and glass skylights.

During the week, the space is relatively quiet, but on Saturdays, the labyrinthine passageways and open courtyards are filled to bursting with foods and wares that would be familiar to Haligonians 200 years ago: vegetables and fruits; breads and meats; flowers and rough-hewn furniture; handmade woolen shirts and knit hats; thick mitts and long scarves. But to this familiar stock is also added modern wares: designer kiosks selling lavender aromatherapy; double-cupped cappuccinos and frothy lattes; modern paintings in oils, pastels, water-colours, and acrylics; painted linoleum kitchen mats and handstitched accordion books; and, of course, a good black coffee served in an enviro-friendly, recycled paper cup.

I gently shift my backside on the uncomfortable cement stair and take another sip of my coffee, still musing on the theory of bitonality. It occurs to me that bitonality may have an historical application, supporting the idea that two, distinct historical moments might exist in the same individual or collective human experience. I wonder for a time if my idea might have usefulness, but then, as I lift my cup to my lips expecting more coffee and realize it's empty, I focus on a more important question: do I need more coffee? A rhetorical question, of course. My theoretical musings will wait.

So I stand, gather my bag, and make my way down the cement

stairs and through the pressing throng, heading to the nearest coffee kiosk. Along the way, as I twist my shoulders between people, I listen to snippets of conversation. There is much talk today of the sensational news – the murder outside a tavern on Argyle Street, a few blocks west of the Farmers' Market, on The Hill. For the last few days, in fact, the newspapers have related the gruesome details to citizens morbidly transfixed by the crime. Admittedly, I too am drawn to the story, partly because I am drawn by parallels with the past – the murder victim was also a young sailor.

According to the stories, a twenty-three-year-old American sailor left a popular downtown tavern – only a few blocks from the old Waterloo site – and witnessed one man beating another man. The sailor didn't hesitate. He stepped in to stop the fight. But one of the men carried a knife.

And he used it.

The young sailor bled to death on the way to the hospital.

Once the initial story dissipates, the newspapers continue their sell-more-papers-sensationalism by presenting the killing as further proof that Halifax is becoming a dangerous city: Halifax, they cry – according to Statistics Canada, the federal agency responsible for collecting such information – has one of the highest crime rates in the country. In muggings and murders, swarmings and assaults, the city ranks at or near the top across the nation. But in truth – newspaper hyperbole aside – this type of violence in Halifax is nothing new.

Halifax has always been a dangerous place.

According to research done by historians Allyson May and Jim Phillips and related in an essay entitled "Homicide in Nova Scotia 1749-1815," the murder rate in late eighteenth- and early nineteenth-century Halifax, compared to other cities its size or even compared to cities far larger, like Boston or London, was outrageously high, one of the highest, in fact. Relative to population, the murder rate in Halifax was nine times higher than any city in the American States and nineteen times higher than the city of London, England. The incident rates for other violent crimes were similarly high.

Why?

According to May and Phillips, it was because the city was filled with soldiers and sailors fueled by alcohol. Halifax was born as a military outpost with no intrinsic reason for being except the prosecution of war. Those who built Halifax, and those who populated it, were inclined, in a sense, to the rhythms of violence. It was no small irony that the city prospered when war raged, filling the streets with dangerous, transient soldiers and sailors, all trained to kill. And it was no small irony that the city floundered when peace emerged, filling the streets with the dangerous desperation born of economic and social hardships.

Angry, frustrated, and dangerous were the natural states of the city.

So too, alcohol was a great elixir for this potential violence. "The business of one half of the town is to sell rum," went one familiar refrain about Halifax, "and the other half to drink it." The crowded conditions and poor economic circumstances of The Hill, conditions exacerbated by alcohol, then combined with the transient sailors and soldiers who had no natural, rooted connection to the community and who, as a consequence of their profession, carried weapons. It was, to put it simply, an explosive combination. The evidence was not just anecdotal. In the late eighteenth and early nineteenth centuries, note May and Phillips, soldiers and sailors committed almost two-thirds of the murders in Halifax – mostly against locals. Halifax, as I have noted, has always been a dangerous place.

After much effort moving through the crowds, I finally reach the coffee kiosk only to stand in a long line that loses itself in a crowd pushing past us toward stalls selling fresh fish and homemade salsa. As I move slowly upstream against the press of people, I think yet again of bitonality: two markets, two sailors, two taverns, two deaths, two ages, but one city. Could a city be like a song with notes existing in two different keys, one in the past and one in the present? Might it somehow explain my belief that the past haunts the present in ways that do not seem obvious?

When I reach the front of the line, I refill my paper cup from a large silver urn and drop some coins into a glass bowl. Then I turn away and head off, travelling with the crowd downstream. Along the way, I stop to taste-test the salsa and sip at my coffee. I think again about the young American sailor and his death, which in turn has me thinking about Alexander Allen, about his autopsy at the Poorhouse, about the many questions that the autopsy answered. Yet I also think about the questions they raised.

In the main courtyard of the market, I find another reasonably comfortable cement stair and sit. I reach into my backpack, remove my notebook, and take out my collection of photocopied newspapers reporting on the death of Alexander Allen. I thumb the pages, running my fingers along the print columns until I find what I am looking for and set aside the other papers. I read from September of 1853: "The death of this comparative stranger has also created a most painful sensation among the citizens, as evidenced by the interest with which the progress of the Inquest has been regarded."

Some things change, and some things stay the same.

Working piecemeal through my notebook and through the newspapers, I reconstruct, to the degree possible, the last eight hours of Alexander Allen's life.

On September 7, 1853, just past five in the evening, sailors gather for shore leave on the deck of the H.M.S. *Cumberland*. The mood is jovial. The chatter is loud and the laughter is contagious. Two rowboats wait at the ship's waterline as a sailor, Able Seaman Alexander Allen, climbs down the rope ladder. Deftly he steps from the rope to the rowboat and takes a seat in the bow. At twenty-five years old, with broad shoulders and a square jaw, Allen cuts a striking figure among his peers. He is taller than most, just under six feet and muscular. His dark curly hair peaks out from under his cap. By all accounts, he is an even-tempered man, not much for drink. His shipmates like and respect him. Says one messmate of Allen's, "He was a very sober, industrious, steady, young man. I never saw him worse for drink." Another describes Allen as "always sober and steady." And yet another says, "He was a steady, sober, and respectable man."

Next down the rope and into the rowboat is Allen's shipmate, James Baldwin. He has known Allen for more than two years. Baldwin nods at Allen as he sits beside him. The two say nothing. Both are distracted by their thoughts, casually watching the other sailors climb down the ladder. These sailors quickly fill the seats in both boats, and as the last sailor takes his seat, they push off. When they pull away from the ship, Alexander Allen reaches into his breeches pocket and pulls out a silver dollar-sized pocket watch. He flips open the cover and glances at the time: it's thirty minutes past five. He shuts the cover and slips the watch back into his breeches pocket. He then looks over his right shoulder to the shore and up The Hill, just making out the flags flying over the fort.

The sailors engage in rowdy conversation. Joseph McCathe and William Giles roughly tease John Davis about his bad luck with women. Davis responds with a rude gesture and a sharp tongue. The sailors laugh. Even Davis smiles. In the middle of the boat, Henry Freeman and Peter Lawrie talk of the taverns they'll visit and of the women they'll see.

The anticipation is palpable.

After ten or fifteen minutes, the boat pulls in against a wharf. The gulls leap up, while dockworkers attend to barrels and crates. One by one, the sailors climb a short ladder to the thick-planked wharf – exactly what time is uncertain. Joseph McCathe remembers that the boat "arrived on shore about six," whereas William Giles recalls it as being "between six and seven." In either case, the sailors climb onto a wharf sometime around six, followed quickly by the second boat. Once the sailors gather at the end of the wharf, advice is given, promises are made, and money is lent. The sailors gather into smaller groups and pairings. Some head south along the waterfront, while others head up the hill toward Barrack Street.

Alexander Allen and William Giles walk together, with Peter Lawrie and Henry Freeman just behind. Henry Freeman recalls that Allen "had a sovereign when he came on shore," a good amount of money for the night. At the foot of Duke Street, Allen tells Giles that he is going up the hill. Giles, Freeman, and Lawrie decide to walk along Water Street toward the Cheapside Market. As Giles remembers, "After going on shore with Allen, I left him. We separated, and I did not see him again until I met him at ten o'clock at the Waterloo." Peter Lawrie remembers the moment, too. "I don't know when

I came on shore," he says. "I take no note of the time. I saw Allen in Duke Street, can't say what time. I was at Young's place first. Again, I don't know what time I went there, but Allen came in after."

Still sitting on the cement stair, I find myself wondering: why did Alexander Allen go off by himself? Nothing was said to suggest why, but I speculate that there may well have been one person he wanted to see. I do know that he walked up Duke Street, probably right to Barrack Street. There, he turned left, and then walked two blocks south, to the Waterloo Tavern, and went inside.

I put down my notebook for a moment and look out at the market crowd, look out at the lively trade in fresh vegetables and community conversation. This moment may well be the only true 'living' connection to an older Halifax, the only historical characteristic of the city not reinvented as stock and trade virtual reality for digital-camera-wearing, cruise ship tourists. Next to me, on the other end of the cement stair, two market patrons eat their chocolate-filled pastries and drink their black coffees. The crowd below me chatters loudly, moving through the courtyard in streams from labyrinth to labyrinth. Some groups of people are caught between the larger streams and small groups, and for a few moments, they form human eddies, swirling until they are picked up again, one-by-one, by a larger stream of people and carried away into the arched stone passageways.

I look behind me and up to a landing above where a young woman plays a squeezebox. She wears jeans, a blue sweatshirt, and a brown brimmed hat. She closes her eyes, swaying as she plays, her music floating ethereally above the chatter. The melody is somehow familiar and somehow not. I know it's old, perhaps some sailor's lament played on an instrument familiar, at the same moment, to this place now and to this place 150 years before. It might well have been a song familiar to Alexander Allen.

I return to my notebook.

By about 6:30 that night, sailor James Baldwin, having walked up George Street and through the Grand Parade to Barrack Street, has already made his way to the Waterloo Tavern. The taproom is quiet, so Baldwin immediately notices Alexander Allen entering. "I recollect the night he lost his life," he later recalls. "I first saw him between the hours of six and seven at Murphy's. He had some ginger beer, and I had some ale. He left the house, and I stayed. I left about seven o'clock, and returned about ten o'clock, remained until about five minutes before eleven o'clock."

What, I wonder, was Allen looking for, and why did he stay so briefly?

Finishing his ginger beer, Allen leaves the Waterloo and walks north, passing two pubs, McClusky's place and the Dog and Duck. A few houses further down, he enters another tavern – Fountain's Place. Inside, a fiddler plays in the corner, and a few patrons dance. After a minute or two, shipmate Anthony Bambridge enters and joins Allen for a drink. "I knew Allen well," said Bambridge. "He was a chum of mine for six months on board the *Cumberland*. I came on shore about half past six, but it was about seven when I got on the hill. I went into Fountain's and saw Allen there. He asked to drink. I took brandy. He took ginger beer. I remained five or ten minutes, went out and left him there."

At the Farmers' Market, the woman with the squeezebox finishes her song. My backside is aching now, so I gather my things into my bag, step up three stairs, and drop a few coins into the squeezebox case. I then walk back down the stairs, into the courtyard. To my left is an odd museum created to honour the Alexander Keith's Brewery of old. Thick wooden beams and two-dozen scattered wooden barrels line the wall. They are somehow meant to suggest an earlier age, but the effect is cheap and contrived. It's obvious that the beams and barrels simply frame up the museum's gift shop and tour entrance. Still, I am intrigued. So with my bag on my shoulder, and coffee in hand, I poke about the gift shop.

Along the wall, I find all forms of beer-themed merchandise: t-shirts, sweatshirts, and coats; ball caps, bracelets, and beer mugs; shot glasses and beer glasses; key chains and bottle openers – and, of course, cases and cases and cases of Keith's beer. Near the cash register, on a hip-high wooden barrel, a large leather guest book sits open. I run my finger down the signatures and place names. Most are trav-

ellers from the United States and Ontario. Their single word comments – great, wonderful, fun, pleasure – seem encouraging enough,
so I consider taking the tour. I step sprightly to the ticket desk, where
a young woman – a twenty-something in jeans, feverishly chewing
gum – talks at a machine-gun pace to another twenty-something, a
young man, who stares fixedly at a newspaper. He says nothing in
response to her chatter, which is probably just as well – he'd be hard
pressed to get a word in.

I clear my throat to get her attention.

The gum chewer turns her head sharply, eyes me suspiciously,
then tilts her head to the side with a look of disapproval.

"Yes," she says between chews.

"Ah, can you tell me about the tour?"

"Yeah, I suppose," she says. Again, she stares at me for a silent
moment, still chewing the gum. "It's a thirty-minute historical reen-
actment of life in Halifax in 1863."

The historical period is spot on, and my writer's interest is piqued.
"That sounds good," I say. "Is there anything else?"

"Well," she says with no enthusiasm, "you then tour a small
brewing operation, and at the end, you get some free beer."

The hour of the morning tempers my normal enthusiasm about
the prospect of free beer, and her lack of enthusiasm about the tour
has me edgy. So I shoot for honesty. "Is it worth it?" I ask.

"Nah," she says bluntly, "except for the free beer." She smiles
while chewing.

"You don't seem too impressed with the place," I say, "except for
the free beer."

She tilts her head to the other side and stares at me for an
uncomfortable moment, trying to decide if my lame joke is worth
a response. "Well, let's just say," she says, "that I'm a disgruntled
employee."

I grin nervously – yet another good argument for strict gun control. I thank her for her time then glance over at the newspaper boy.
"Poor bugger," I mutter.

I leave the Keith's Beer gift shop. I lift my coffee to my lips
only to realize my cup is empty again. But feeling jangled by the caf-

feine, or maybe by the disgruntled gum chewer, I decide not to refill. Besides, it's time to go. So I leave the courtyard and walk through an arched passage, and stride east to the exit. Outside, the air is the cool, but the sun is shining. I pull my Red Sox cap over my head and walk south along Lower Water Street, passing the outdoor kiosks selling large two-foot-high, wooden mushroom stools and one-foot-long, pine-board wall-hangings painted with Scottish clan names and tartans. Further down, for two blocks, modern buildings rise on both sides of the street with paved parking lots in between. On the left, in front of a hotel construction site, a new bronze plaque sits in a thick, squared piece of stone and granite. It announces the Alexander Keith's Brewery District.

The plaque summarizes the career of Alexander Keith, who, like so many business magnates of the Industrial Age, moved deftly from big money born of vice to big politics born of vice. Bankrolled by barrels of beer money, Alexander Keith was an unexceptional three-term mayor of Halifax from 1843 to 1853. I muse that a mile or so to the west, in the Camp Hill Cemetery, his remains share the earth with arguably the most famous Nova Scotian, Joseph Howe. But it is Keith, not Howe, who gets all the attention.

As with the famous Paris gravesite of rock and roll musician Jim Morrison in Pere Lachaise cemetery, Alexander Keith's gravestone has become a perverse, late-night, drunken pilgrimage site, a symbol of youthful excess – Nova Scotia style. On any given morning through-out the year – and particularly around Alexander Keith's October 5th birthday – one can find as many as a dozen or more Keith's beer bottles carefully perched on the base of Keith's tombstone – a tower-ing red granite obelisk. Adding to the irony, the city (or the cemetery) has built a large wooden map that indicates the general layout of the graveyard and the relative location of all the gravestones. A single, siz-able star identifies Alexander Keith's gravesite – and that's it. Old Joe Howe's white, weather-beaten, granite tombstone stands just a dozen yards or so away, under an old, bent tree, all but forgotten.

Reading the bronze plaque on Lower Water Street, I can't help but think the city is yet again recasting its dubious past, moving away from plebian farmers' markets and ambitious beer moguls, to official business districts and heralded patrician mayors – just another version of changing Barrack Street to Brunswick Street, I suppose.

At Fountain's Place, Alexander Allen finishes his ginger beer and decides to leave. He walks north to Prince Street. There, he turns right, walks a block, and turns right again on Albemarle Street. Just a few houses down, he enters Mitty Johnson's place. From two contradictory accounts, the time is between seven and eight.

Mitty Johnson's place is lively, filled with sailors and soldiers – two groups who rarely got on well, particularly when liquor was involved. Allen's shipmate Anthony Bambridge describes what happened there. "I saw Allen at about eight or half past eight, in Mitty Johnson's," he says. "There was a row in Johnson's between soldiers and sailors. They can never agree. There were blows struck with sticks. Allen jumped in. He was a very strong man, you know, thickset. I said to him that I would fight for him to the last drop of my blood. And we cleared ourselves." Was Allen injured in the fight? Nothing was noted by his shipmates. Still, blows were struck with sticks. Perhaps Allen was swift and strong enough to avoid being injured. Perhaps Bambridge exaggerated the story, with perhaps more curses thrown than punches. In any case, no one else mentions the fight.

Following that altercation, it is unclear where Allen goes next. Probably, like the other sailors, he moves from tavern to tavern. Shipmate William Giles suggests that Allen made contact with the prostitute Sarah Myers at this time. As Giles recalls, "Allen told me that at eight o'clock in the evening, Sarah Myers had taken his hat from him, and that he intended to go back for it." But Giles may have been mistaken about the event or the time or both. No one at the Waterloo remembers seeing Allen between 6:30 and ten o'clock. Myers herself makes no mention of seeing Allen at eight o'clock or of taking the hat earlier in the evening, saying, "I saw Allen at the Waterloo on that Wednesday night about 6:15, the first time he came in. He was a short time there and went out again."

Tavern owner Richard McCabe saw Allen that night, too. "Allen was at my house on Albemarle Street on the night before his death, a little before nine," he recalls. "He never drank any intoxicating drink at my house," McCabe adds interestingly. "Indeed, he told me that he had made a resolution to drink no liquor before the ship arrived home and was discharged. He told me that he was very contrary when in liquor, that it brought him many troubles, which he never got in sober."

I leave the bronze plaque dedicated to Alexander Keith and cut across Lower Water Street and through a parking lot. I make my way to the waterfront, then turn north and walk on for a stretch. Most of this area is now given over to expensive condominiums for couples without children and to tourist traps for cruise ship crowds with an hour and a half on their hands. The dozen or so wharves in the area are still used by incoming boats and yachts and a couple of early twentieth-century museum ships. On my right, I pass an enormous blue wave sculpture rising up out of the cement. The sculpture looks more like a large blue cement tongue petulantly sticking itself out at passers-by. I wonder if the sculptor had a sly sense of humour and a modest antipathy towards tourists.

Further along the waterfront, I pass more shops hawking t-shirts and trinkets, kiosks selling flat cinnamon-coated, chocolate-covered pastries and twenty flavours of ice-cream, and a wooden shed promoting amphibious tours of the city and harbour. Still further along, on my left, I pass a parking lot where the city's first gallows once stood – that tall hardwood tree from which Peter Carteel was hanged. Needless to say, there is nothing erected to mark this site. On my right, I pass a terminal building, where a blue and white ferry spews blue and white smoke from its engines, as it prepares to leave for the Dartmouth shore. Along with the Farmers' Market, this ferry is also a living link to the past – the oldest continuing saltwater ferry in the world.

A dozen yards further along a brick path, I find myself among a collection of old stone warehouses, many of which would have been familiar to Alexander Keith and to Alexander Allen. These warehouses once contained goods of the world – received, stored, and shipped. During the War of 1812, legalized piracy filled these warehouses to the rafters with privateers' booty. Indeed, for more than a hundred years this space was the nexus of Halifax business, the city's heartbeat, replete with people and sounds and smells. But by the 1960s, with the Age of Sail long passed, these old warehouses had fallen into decrepit disrepair, more a home for wharf rats than dry goods. So in the name of urban renewal, the city tried to level them. But unlike the easy yielding of street names, the old stone walls of the warehouses ignored the wrecking ball, bouncing it harmlessly away. The forgotten buildings were again remembered by the citizens of Halifax, who raised a mighty ruckus. Unable to knock down the walls, the politicians tacked and took credit for staying an execution, duly recasting the area as Historic Properties, with a new role as virtual history selling plastic lobsters and tartaned shot glasses.

I walk inside the main building of Historic Properties, down a long, wide corridor with shops on either side selling maps and sweaters, haircuts and dresses, and flowers pressed between glass. At the end of the mall, a food court opens onto the waterfront boardwalk, and beyond that, the harbour. With the hour now comfortably past twelve, I stop to eat. In this upscale food court, I order myself a veggie wrap and designer P.E.I. potato french-fries. I then sit, with my red cafeteria tray, at a table overlooking the harbour. During these cool months, glass garage doors slide down to protect the food court from the weather.

Thirsty, I leave my food at the table and walk a half-dozen yards to a microbrewery called John Shippy's. The name is apt for the area. On July 17, 1749, just days after the city's founding, John Shippy applied for, and received, the first license for a tavern in Halifax. Shippy's tavern was, of course, followed by many, many more. I eschew my typical Rickard's Red and opt for the beer brewed in the copper cauldrons above. The stone-faced clerk pours my drink and takes my money – seven dollars for a pint. I grumble about the tourist price, but the clerk is unmoved and hands me my change for a ten. So I take my seven-dollar pint and return to my seat and eat my veggie wrap.

Taking my first bite, I look out at the harbour and watch a container ship passing by. I consider that the lively life of this harbour might also be another living connection to the past. Aside from a naval presence of a dozen aged and rumpled grey ships, and the country's entire fleet of four perennially leaky submarines, the harbour is largely given over to business and pleasure boats. In the warm months, all forms of tourist boats chug about: a half dozen amphibious vehicles on land and water; a tugboat refitted to look like a popular kid's television character, complete with a huge red ball cap and two enormous moving eyes on the smokestack; an old steel fishing boat refitted with two masts to suggest the Age of Sail, which fools only tourists and drunks; and an amusingly misplaced New Orleans style riverboat.

In front of me, on the other side of the garage door glass, a single grey-winged seagull struts along the boardwalk. In the warm months, the boardwalk is filled with tables and tourists, and so, of course, the gulls are regulars, poking about where kids spill french-fries. But this lonely gull is out of season. He carefully looks around, darting his beak at the odd bits of garbage. After a minute or two, he realizes that nothing is to be gained here. He takes a running start at the boardwalk's edge, then launches himself over the water and into the air.

At the table, I have a sip of my seven-dollar beer and open my notebook.

"I next saw him a little before ten o'clock," remembers Allen's messmate James Baldwin, "at the corner of the Dog and Duck. It is a shanty well known and kept by Abraham Provost, just north of the Waterloo. Allen was sober when I left him at Provost's." Again, Allen enters and exits a tavern, spending little time. Is he looking for someone? Allen leaves the Dog and Duck not long after Baldwin, probably around ten o'clock. He then heads north to Prince Street, turns east one block, and walks south along Albemarle Street until he arrives at Young's place. There, he opens a door, which brushes over a copper bell announcing his arrival.

The owner, Samuel Young, remembers Allen coming into his shop. "I kept shop in Albemarle Street," he recalls. "I knew Alexander Allen. He came to my shop about a quarter past ten. I knew the hour from looking at my clock. He came there to look after Margaret Murphy. He asked me to tell her that he wished to see her. I did so. I went into the taproom and found her in company with Peter Lawrie. When Margaret Murphy came out to Allen, he asked her if she would have anything to drink. She said she would and took a glass of brandy. They talked for a moment, took a glass of brandy and both went out."

I look up from my notebook and stare out at the harbour. Margaret Murphy was Thomas Murphy's estranged wife. What was the relationship here? What was said between Margaret Murphy and Allen? Why had they left the tavern? Where were they going? I look back at the notebook. "I had no other women in the house but Margaret Murphy," says Young. "She told me she lived at Abraham Provost's, which was a common brothel. She was a common prostitute and addicted to drinking. Indeed, she is more addicted to drinking than other women of that class."

When the copper doorbell rings again, Peter Lawrie realizes what has happened. He gets up from his table, opens the door, and enters the street, following after Allen and Murphy. There, the couple has only managed to walk a dozen yards or so, north. Lawrie yells a challenge at Allen, who stops, turns, and faces Lawrie. "Yes, when Lawrie heard the bell ring," confirms Young, "he went out and they commenced fighting in the alleyway. I saw Lawrie knock Allen down. His face was cut somewhat – but not seriously. They both entered the house afterwards, and they made friends. It was about twenty minutes to eleven o'clock. Allen's face was bloody, so stained with blood, in fact, that anyone could discern it. And from a quarter past ten till eleven o'clock he was at my house with his face bloodied. He said he would not wash himself. He would go where he had agreed to stay all night and wash himself there. I stayed talking to Allen until eleven o'clock. The clock struck eleven while I was talking to him."

Peter Lawrie is careful to describe the fight as brief and the anger short-lived. "There was a scuffle between us – blood came from him – it must have been from his nose," he reflects. "Sure, I knocked him down once I believe, but he was seen well afterwards, and we parted friends." After a moment, he adds, "After the fight, Allen remained two or three minutes more in Young's, then he left. I continued with

Margaret Murphy that night." By Lawrie's description, the fight was a non-event, but two other witnesses, locals who passed by in the street that night, suggest otherwise.

William Newcomb lives in Halifax and recollects the night Allen was killed. "I left Mr. Hatch's house – where I was staying at the time – about ten. As I went along northward, there was a man lying in the drain. By then, it was about twenty minutes past ten," he remembers. "The man, Allen, was lying there in the gutter. I thought at first he had been taking liquor, but when he was up for some time he appeared steady. The blood was running down his forehead."

When asked if the blood was from above the eye or else where, Newcomb says, "I could not say that blood was running from beneath his hair." Then Newcomb has more to say. "When he first raised," he adds thoughtfully, "Allen staggered a little. It might have been from a severe fall. After all, a high curb is there. The blood was quite plain upon his face."

At my table, I have another sip of beer and consider the description. Then, with my pencil, I underline the observation.

Newcomb continues, "I lifted him up, and he appeared perfectly steady."

At that moment, from the door of Young's place, Margaret Murphy appears. "Come in, Allen, and wash your face," she says, "and I'll dare him to strike you again." Lawrie feels Murphy's provocation and rushes again at Allen, striking him. They both fall to the road, locked together. The scuffle only lasts a minute longer before those standing and watching part them.

Newcomb holds Lawrie by the shoulders, looking him in the eyes. "Are you not his comrade?" he asks.

Lawrie looks away from Allen to Newcomb, silent for a moment. "He's not only my chum," Lawrie finally says, "but he's my messmate."

"Well, you should be ashamed," says Newcomb.

"But," protests Lawrie, pointing his finger at Allen, "he took away a woman I had, and I must have some revenge."

Newcomb later notes that Allen "had a small cut on his forehead" but felt it was "nothing to cause death."

Another local, James O'Donnell, also sees the fight. He remembers it this way: "I lived in Albemarle Street. I heard the row first in my house, only a couple of yards off. So I had a look. That was when I saw a fight opposite Samuel Young's place. I saw Allen knocked down and lay in the gutter. He could stand as soon as he was raised up and put on the platform. But he did seem a little stupid, and he fell again, without, it seemed, the other striking him."

As before, I underline the comments: "… seemed a little stupid …", "… fell again without, it seemed, the other striking him …"

O'Donnell continues, "He said the other man had the advantage of him. I understood he meant that Allen was in liquor. There was a crowd round when he was laying down, and there was a wooden curb. He was picked up and he and the other had a round or two after. Again, he had a scratch over his eye and it bled a little. I did not think there was anything serious that evening." In every description – from those at the fight and from those later at the Waterloo – the cut over Allen's eye was minor. "I saw him go away, sober," reports O'Donnell. "I think it was near eleven o'clock. On the next day, the cut over the eye of the dead man I saw was a more severe one. The night was not very dark. I was within a few feet of the man when he was raised up, and I took particular notice of the wound. It was a mere scratch."

I push the cafeteria tray to the top of the table, and then have a good sip at my beer. I sit back and think. I am troubled by the reports of the fight. Certainly, witnesses do remember the same event differently, but clearly Lawrie felt he was under some suspicion, repeatedly stating that the fight was brief, without consequence, and that the two had parted as friends. The tavern owner, Young, supported Lawrie's statement. But if that were the case, it certainly would be unlike any fight I had seen. On the other hand, the two witnesses suggest that Allen was worse off, that Allen appeared disoriented, whether from Lawrie's fist or from the wooden curb. I become more suspicious of Lawrie when, after picking up the paper and reading more testimony, I consider the aspersions Lawrie cast at Thomas Murphy.

"I saw Allen several times at the Waterloo," Lawrie recalls, "where Thomas Murphy refused to draw him liquor and once he said he would give Allen what he had promised him a long time ago. This was the summer before last. I don't believe he was there last summer until the night he was killed. Indeed, I have seen Murphy refuse him liquor the summer before last, and tell him to go out of his house."

Here, Lawrie provides a ready-made threat from Murphy. Then Lawrie adds motive by saying, "Allen was cohabitating with Murphy's wife at this time. Murphy showed a feeling of dislike to Allen twice. Allen was aware that Murphy was inveterate against him." But then Lawrie u-turns and distances himself from the suggestion. "I know of no quarrel between Murphy and Allen. I know of no reason why Murphy refused Allen liquor." Lawrie casts the aspersion, then retracts it – but the damage is done, and the spotlight is turned from him.

After the fight, around 10:45, Alexander Allen, with blood still on his face, leaves Young's place on Albemarle and walks the block back to Barrack Street, to the Waterloo, where Anthony Bambridge sees him enter. "I saw him at about eleven in the Waterloo," he says. "It was quiet, as there was no fiddler playing. Giles came out with me. Allen appeared quite sober and had no marks on marks on his face. Later, I saw him standing at the bar talking in a friendly way to Murphy. I also saw Gordon sitting against the room they dine in. There were no women there." I consider his comments about seeing no marks on Allen's face, but then I read this: "Although Giles was not drunk," Bambridge says, "I was well in for liquor."

Was he too drunk to remember or to see?

William Giles confirms Bambridge's story, but he also gives some credence to a conflict between Allen and Murphy. "I met him at ten o'clock at the Waterloo," remembers Giles. "He drank nothing but ginger beer and was sober when I left about a quarter of an hour after." Giles recalls that the fiddler, Shortis, was playing, and that both he and Allen danced. After that, overheated, the two step to the bar, where Allen offers to treat Murphy's housekeeper, Mary Anne Cole, to a glass of brandy. Cole agrees, but behind the counter, Thomas Murphy glares. "Why do you take that," he says to Cole, "when you can get plenty?"

Cole shrugs and downs the glass of brandy. She turns and smiles coyly.

Murphy then glares at Allen.

"What are you looking at me for?" Allen asks. "Do I owe you anything?"

Further words are exchanged. Giles recalls Murphy saying, "Clear out, or by God I'll give you what I promised you six weeks past."

"She's only a damned whore," Allen shoots back, ending the conversation and walking away from Murphy and crossing the tavern to sit with Sarah Myers.

Giles says he left the Waterloo around eleven o'clock. "I left Allen with Sarah Myers," he says. "I saw Gordon there and Murphy. So too, I saw Ballard, Myers, and Cole. But the only girl I saw him with after buying Cole a brandy was Sarah Myers." Giles was the last of Allen's shipmates to see him alive. As with Bambridge, I note that his memory of the event may be suspect. "If Allen's face had been bloody or scratched," he claims, "I must have noticed them. But I saw none."

On the other side of the glass garage window, I watch a piece of paper blow by in the wind. It loops once, lifts high, and then drops over the edge of the wharf into the water. I struggle to reconcile the stories of Bambridge and Giles with those of Lawrie, O'Donnell, and Newcomb. Finally, I decide that Giles and Bambridge must simply be wrong. Too many saw the blood on Allen's face. It had to be there. Confident in that thought, I finish the remainder of my beer and place the empty glass on the cafeteria tray. I stand, stuffing my notebook and papers into my backpack and head to the door. The temperature outside has dropped with the afternoon sun, and I involuntarily shiver as I pull on my ball cap and start walking along the boardwalk. In the thick of the city's tourist trade, among the stone shells of the old privateers' warehouses, I review the day. I review the threads that still connect the city's past to its present, the threads that still run through the city's historic fabric – the Farmers' Market, the waterfront, even the violence. In a sense, they each provide a variation on historic bitonality, each offering discordant notes in different historical keys, but all playing the same song.

So too I consider the last hours of Alexander Allen. I imagine him sitting, bloodied, talking with Sarah Myers in the Waterloo taproom. It's near midnight by then, of course. That's when Murphy, seeing the blood again on Allen's face, tells Sarah Myers to take him upstairs and clean him up. And with that, I am back where I began – minutes before Allen's death in the Waterloo Tavern.

Having worked through the stories, having reviewed the autopsy, and having walked through Allen's last day, I still wonder: why would Allen jump from the window? But perhaps that is the wrong question. Perhaps the better questions are these: How did Alexander Allen die? What was it that Dr. Allan said at the autopsy? That a serious blow to the head could have a delayed response, that death could be triggered by an earlier accident – like a blow against a wooden curb, perhaps? If Allen jumped from the window, might he have triggered the death already in process? If so, then was Lawrie possibly guilty of Allen's death? And would that explain why Lawrie talked up tales of revenge and a tense relationship with an estranged wife?

Or was there more to consider?

There was, of course, one discordant story about that night – that emotional outburst from Mary Anne Cole to the jailor on the night of Allen's death, an outburst that was quickly recanted – but one that offered a very different story of September 7 and 8, 1853.

A story shared between two prostitutes and one politician – Matilda Ballard, Sarah Myers, and Joseph Howe.

Chapter 9

The Witnesses

In 1859, after years spent reviewing observations from around the world and across a thousand years of time, German astronomer Gustav Spoerer proudly presented to the scientific community his Spoerer's Law, which posited that sunspots – those regions on the surface of the sun characterized by lower temperatures and intense magnetic activity – occur in predictable, systematic cycles. As one might expect with a sweeping theory of such galactic size, the scientific community carefully reviewed Spoerer's findings only to respond with bemused silence when none who reviewed it managed to decipher what, exactly, Spoerer's Law had to do with anything. Gustav Spoerer and his law of predictable sunspots might well have been forgotten by history altogether had it not been for another astronomer, an Englishman named Edward Walter Maunder, who – some thirty-five years later – used Spoerer's Law to support his own theory: The Maunder Minimum.

The Maunder Minimum argued that a precipitous drop in solar spot activity between 1645 and 1715 had a causal relationship to the concurrent Little Ice Age in Europe. In addition to explaining why everyone in Europe had been so bloody cold for four generations, the

Maunder Minimum more importantly became one of the first celestial events scientifically proven to have had a direct effect on the Earth, and perhaps one of the most important – save, of course, for the odd, gigantic meteor that collides with the planet, effectively wiping out 300 million years of dinosaur domination and evolution. The point, here, is that for the nineteenth-century mind, Spoerer's Law and The Maunder Minimum replaced – with substantive science and careful study – the ancient superstitions about dark omens born of solar eclipses and shooting stars.

That, or it just confirmed them.

Either way, I find myself considering the Maunder Minimum, shooting stars, and dark omens as I stroll through the narrow alley-way between two warehouses in the waterfront Historic Properties. The dark-grey stone walls and the weather-beaten wooden shingles and even the deep-set granite-framed windows tangibly play with my sense of time and place, sliding me gently between the past and the present. So too I think of the past because somewhere above me, in late August of 1853, just two weeks before Alexander Allen died, a Halifax newspaper reported that a "splendid meteor apparently nearly half the size of the moon was observed by many persons of the east ward of the city about quarter past eight on Sunday evening last. Its descent was very slow and irregular or oscillating. In colour, it resem-bled the pale light of the moon and had a very beautiful appearance." I think about that meteor flying overhead, oscillating slowly though the atmosphere, and I imagine those who, in 1853, watch the meteor with fascination and maybe some trepidation at the waterfront and up on The Hill. And not without reason, I wonder if two women at the Waterloo Tavern – the part-time prostitutes, Sarah Myers and Matilda Ballard – watch the meteor that night, watch its oscillating light shimmer on the undulating harbour water below.

And if they did, would they have thought it a bad omen?

I exit the alleyway at a spot where, in 1789, the Jerusalem Coffee House once stood, until destroyed by a fire in 1837. There, I dart across the tail end of Upper Water Street where the road bottlenecks to accommodate a large, six-storey building of irregular-shaped grey stone. Built in 1841, the building was, coincidentally enough, named the Jerusalem Warehouse, perhaps in memory of the long-standing, popular coffee shop. In 1870, the building was – in light irony – renamed the Morse's Teas building, and two more stories of red brick were added to the top. Today, the faded red and white letters of MORSES'S TEAS run across the fifth and sixth floors of the building facing north.

From the sidewalk at the east side of the building, I turn right along the south side, into a small pedestrian passageway where eight wide, well-worn, wooden stairs climb to Hollis Street. On the third stair, I stop and look up at the building's stone face, rising ominously, windowless, six floors up. I then look down at the base of the wall and glance at a grey door recessed in the shadows. To my left, at the top of the stairs on grey bricks, there sits an old, black ship's anchor bolted firmly to the wall by black linked chain. In a stream-of-consciousness connection, the combination of grey stones and black chains reminds me of prison, which in turn reminds me of the Waterloo prisoners. So I take a seat at the right side of one wooden step – in this passageway that would have been familiar to the citizens walking the streets of the waterfront in 1853 – and I momentarily lose myself in the past, thinking of those arrested and jailed after that night at the Waterloo.

The jailor, James Wilson, remembers well the fate of the prisoners after the Coroner's Inquest. "Sarah Myers and Matilda Ballard were committed to jail on a writ detainer," he recalls. "Thomas Murphy, John Gordon, and David Parsons were also committed to jail under a murder warrant. About three weeks later, these three were removed to the penitentiary by order of the Board of Works, while Cole, Myers, and Ballard continued in my custody as charged with willful murder."

Sitting on my wooden stair, I recall that the penitentiary where Gordon, Parsons, and Murphy are sent was situated west of the downtown. But the jail where Myers, Cole, Ballard, Gordon, Parsons, and Murphy are first interned was located just next to the Poorhouse, the "death house" as Dr. Allan called it, where Alexander Allen's body was autopsied. Just prior to the prisoners arriving at the jail, the body is taken from the Poorhouse in a plain pine casket, loaded into an open cart, and pulled by horse some two miles north, to the Naval Hospital Graveyard. There, with little fanfare, Alexander Allen is buried.

That night, on September 9, as the prisoners enter the jail, James Wilson recognizes Mary Anne Cole. Her family is known to Wilson. As he recalls, Cole's shoulders are slumped and her head is down. As she passes, Wilson calls her by name. "Mary," he says, "has it come to this at last?"

Cole looks up. She recognizes Wilson and bursts out crying. "I had nothing to do with it," she sobs. "I was in Tom's room when they were upstairs killing the man."

Wilson recalls the statement clearly, and also recalls her recanting. "She denied using this expression the following day," he says, "but I am confident that these were the words she used."

Cole's brief outburst remains the only discordant fragment in the many tales told of the events that evening – until six weeks later. James Wilson recalls how the story, with stark suddenness, turned on its head. "Six weeks after committal," he says, "the women were in my custody, not as prisoners, but as Queen's evidence."

What happened after six weeks in the jail? Ballard and Myers abruptly changed their testimony. Both flatly accused Thomas Murphy and John Gordon of willful murder. "They were turned over as Queen's evidence," Wilson says, "on the authority of the Provincial Secretary from which time they were allowed more liberty. They were permitted to go into my kitchen and mess [eat] with my family. Myers acted as my servant and was paid wages. Previously they were confined separately upstairs. Mary Anne Cole was confined in the end of the jail, and Myers and Ballard were confined in rooms separated by a passage. My orders were at first that these women were to speak to no one, and if they did, no answer was to be returned. I received these orders principally through Mr. Howe. If any person brought a message to them I would deliver it and get their answer. I had orders that their legal advisors should have free admission to them."

Why, I wonder, after all that time, did Myers and Ballard change their story? Was it the pressure of guilt? The promise of reward? The pain of coercion? It's worth noting that at the trial in April, the jailor, James Wilson, calls Mary Anne Cole "an unyielding, unbending bitch." He also finds himself having to deny rumours of rough coercion. "I never caused strange and unnatural noises to be made near Mary Cole's room to alarm her," he says under questioning. "I never told Sarah Myers or Matilda Ballard that if they did not make a confession to implicate Gordon and Murphy they would put it on them." The source of such accusations is unknown, lost to history, but Wilson's vehement denials raise questions about his character and the events that occur at the jail.

So why did they change their story?

Perhaps the women changed their tales under the persuasive power of Joseph Howe. In 1853, Joe Howe is asked to play a role in this notorious case, even though he is, at that time, working for the private sector in another progressive cause, building the Nova Scotia railroad. As he recalls, "My first visit to the jail was made pursuant to the instructions of the Lieutenant-Governor in consequence of a complaint made by the Admiral that the prison was not sufficiently secure. On examination, I found that four of the prisoners were on the ground floor. They could communicate with each other by the opening through the door. It was therefore suggested that, for the additional accommodation, they should be sent to the Penitentiary and in company with the sheriff. I waited on his lordship, the Chief Justice, and he sanctioned their removal, intimating, however, that the sheriff would still be liable for their safe custody. I am not aware of visiting the jail subsequently until sent for by the prisoners when the girl Myers made a statement which left the impression on my mind that she had more to tell. What she did say at first was not sufficient to make action on my part necessary. She subsequently made a more ample confession, which was confirmed by the girl Ballard. I afterward communicated with the girl Cole, whose family I had known previously, and with the coloured man, giving them to understand what the nature of the confession was which Ballard and Myers had made."

It is clear that Joseph Howe's initial visit made a lasting impression on both Sarah Myers and Matilda Ballard. And vice versa. Both women said something at the initial visit that encouraged Joe Howe to return. Perhaps, in some sense, Howe was still the old newspaper reporter, unable to resist a good lead. "I said nothing to induce the confession made by the girls," he adds, somewhat defensively. "I made them no promise. The expression first used by Myers was 'I wish those who know all about it would tell and relieve those not guilty.' I don't think I visited the jail more than twice afterwards. I went to the extent of assuring the girls that, in the event of their telling all they know, they would be protected by the Government from injury. I also saw Parsons at the Penitentiary. The statement of the girls did not implicate him. I don't recollect what I said to Parsons. When I first visited the prison the girls were under the impression they would be released almost immediately. I made such statements as entirely destroyed such belief. I told Parsons it was better that he should disclose all he knew about the transaction."

The jailor, James Wilson, corroborates Howe's account. "Mr. Howe came into the jail as Provincial Secretary and head crown officer," he recalls. "He was there four or five times, and the girls were introduced to him sometimes above and sometimes below. He visited the girls very soon after they were placed in my custody and continued to visit them until the time they gave him some confession. Mr. Howe had been there three times before that."

My wooden stair in the pedestrian passageway is becoming uncomfortable, so I stand, turn, and walk up the remaining steps to the street. At the top, I take a left, passing two granite buildings also built in the early nineteenth century, also sites familiar to passing citizens of 1853, and continue one block south along Hollis Street.

Hollis Street has always been a paradoxical microcosm of the city itself. It was once the main street of the city, with the Lieutenant-Governor's house, Province House, numerous well-to-do merchants' homes, the haughty Halifax Club, the post office, posh hotels, banks, and insurance companies all facing the street. Yet also facing the street was the Cheapside Market, Alexander Keith's Brewery, and a series of infamous bordellos. The grand variety and stretch of social rank along Hollis Street spoke to the strange, symbiotic relationship of classes and values in this city – and also its tensions or pretensions. It was no accident that the Lieutenant-Governor's mansion ultimately changed its entrance to face west, to Barrington Street, turning its back forever on the lower orders of Hollis Street. These lower orders continued to be part of Hollis Street's rich social mix even as recently as ten years ago when, at the far end of the road, prostitutes still strolled Cornwallis Park looking for business from the locals and from visiting sailors, under the stern gaze of Edward Cornwallis's bronze statue.

As I consider the life of the lower orders on Hollis Street, I think it's no surprise that Matilda Ballard and Sarah Myers were treated with such suspicion, even derision, by the authorities when they changed their stories. As a group, working-class women in 1853 lived hard lives with little hope, relying on patience and perseverance. This was perhaps even truer of those living and working on Barrack Street. Certainly, prostitutes like Sarah Myers, Mary Anne Cole, and Matilda Ballard would have needed a good deal of patience and perseverance to survive.

In my notebook, I have copied the text of an advertisement, of all things, from a newspaper printed about the same time as the meteor appeared over the east ward of the city. It reads: "A correspondent at Sheet Harbour says James Cameron, fisherman of Pope's Harbour, recently picked up the body of a woman at sea. The remains were decently interred on shore. From appearances, the woman had been murdered – probably by a blow over the forehead. She had nothing on but her nightdress, a flannel petticoat, and a cotton ditto flowered at the bottom. She was barefooted and barelegged, but very decent and had not apparently been more than twenty-four hours in the water. She has long black hair and is not a native of our shore. I think you had better advertise her in the newspapers. It is clear there is something wrong. She is not known anywhere about our shore. I think she has been ill used by some ruffian and thrown overboard."

The casual tone of the letter says much. Women were often enough "ill used." No doubt the endemic nature of prostitution in Halifax, a port city thick with transient sailors and soldiers and fast-flowing rum, shaped the darker perceptions of women in the working-class. Certainly, prostitution was widespread in 1850s Halifax; how widespread, though, is difficult to know. By comparison, in London, England, in 1841, according to estimates by historian Megara Bell – in her work "The Fallen Women in Fiction and Legislation" – as many as 80,000 prostitutes worked in a city of two million people. Estimates by historian Judith Walkowitz suggest that for a typical mid-nineteenth-century city in England or North America there would have been one prostitute for every dozen men. So it seems likely enough, given its dark history as a rowdy garrison town, Halifax's ratio of prostitutes to adult males might well have been higher.

This statistic may not be as shocking as it first seems. The underground nature of prostitution, particularly in the Golden Age of Sail, was socially and economically complex. As Megara Bell notes, the Dickensian image of prostitutes as fallen angels, who descend, spiraling, into destitution and depravity, was more fiction than fact. In truth, women who became prostitutes in that period did so, more often than not, to escape a pervasive, grinding poverty. Typically, women who became prostitutes were single, between the ages of eighteen and twenty-two. Before becoming prostitutes, these women often worked as maids, housekeepers, or cooks. In these jobs, they worked fourteen-hour days in poor conditions and received poor wages. Many of these women would continue in these professions and use prostitution as a part-time pursuit. Paradoxically, prostitution provided women with higher incomes and, in some cases, even better working conditions. Through prostitution, many women could afford their own rooms, their own clothes, and an independence not otherwise attainable for women in conventional positions. So, too, in a time of strict social and political taboos, these women could participate in the rich social and political life of the tavern.

Counter to the Dickensian caricature, according to Bell, prostitution was often a transitional occupation – of course, not one without serious, life-threatening risks and dangers. But for those women who avoided physical abuse, alcohol addiction, and debilitating disease, marriage and a modest settled life was a reasonable expectation.

The harsh social condemnation of prostitution, like that of drinking, was on the whole the expression of the middle and upper classes, of those who controlled the newspapers and the politics, of those whose own vices were affordably hidden. But among the working classes, particularly on Barrack Street, prostitution, like drinking, was more complex – neither accepted nor rejected. That said, prostitutes were seen by all classes – as were sailors in some respects – as outsiders. So, when Matilda Ballard and Sarah Myers changed their stories, they faced the angry incredulity of men from the middling and upper classes: the judge, the lawyers, and even the jury who sat with harsh opinions of their character and their profession – their tales suspicious until proven otherwise.

I'm pondering nineteenth-century prostitutes as I turn right on the corner of Duke Street, where in the 1760s the Crown Coffee House was located, and where in 1767 one of many treaties with the Mi'kmaq was signed. From there, I walk a block north and turn right onto Granville Street. I stroll between two, large stone lions, standing on their hind legs and holding shields in their forelegs to protect the entrance to an outdoor pedestrian mall of brick and cobblestone. Granville Street is another of the original streets of the city. However, unlike modern day Hollis Street, where once it was a lively stretch of homes and businesses, today its blocks offer the traveller little more than the back-end of large brick buildings and garbage-filled parking lots. But in this last block, at the north end of the street, there remains a visually stunning collection of late nineteenth-century buildings, raised from the ashes of a great fire in October of 1859, a fire which destroyed a large portion of the downtown.

The *Illustrated London News* reported the event: "At nine o'clock on the night of the 9th of September the little metropolis of the province of Nova Scotia was startled by the unwelcome sound of the fire-bells. Soon it became known that the flames were at work in the very centre of its budding magnificence, and with a fury that bade defiance to all counter-efforts. Houses and stores, wooden, brick, and stone, all alike fed the flames, until, of the two extensive blocks touching on Hollis and Barrington Streets, with Granville Street (the Haligonian's paradise), running betwixt them, nothing escaped except one store, by saving which, by the way, the fire was prevented spreading over the town. The damage is considerable – about £200,000; the insurance covers £131,000 of the loss. Sixty of the finest buildings in Halifax, covering four acres of ground, were destroyed; two lives were also lost, and many persons received severe injuries. From the brilliant play of colours caused by the combustion of the inflammable materials with which it was filled, and from the danger caused by the proximity of the Ordnance Magazine, the excitement here was intense."

The four-storey granite and sandstone buildings that rose from the ashes of the 1859 fire project a grand elegance with their arched and pillared windows above large, open, ground level storefronts. The upper floors on the east side are mostly occupied by the Nova Scotia College of Art and Design, while the upper floors to the west side belong to a chain hotel. The ground floors along both sides of the street present an attractive combination of lively taverns and trendy shops. About a quarter of the way along, on the west side, across from a small stone fountain, I see a modernist sculpture of a large, twisted, steel cup – a twenty-first century Jerusalem Coffeehouse.

The coffeehouses of seventeenth- and eighteenth-century London were sometimes called "penny universities" – presumably for the cheapness of the coffee and the quality of the conversation. Such coffeehouses had a long and rich history as literary, business, and political venues. So too, in early Halifax, the coffeehouse, as with the tavern, was something of a social, political, and economic nexus. Even today, the Halifax coffeehouse remains a vibrant cultural hub with shops catering to all subcultures and social groups. I enter this one and walk to the counter, not far from the door.

The décor is typical postmodern: a culture-cornucopia overlaid with past-and-present bric-a-brac. Despite overlooking the beautiful nineteenth-century buildings of the Art College, the inside ignores this context and is painted in three bold colours: silver, red, and yellow. The world music playing on the stereo – its staccato rhythms at once Spanish but also African – is just loud enough to mask the constant hum of the air exchange ductwork. Just above my head, on thick grey wires, hangs a wooden racing scull inexplicably cut into two pieces of six or eight feet. Two blue, wooden oars are attached on either side of the scull's front half.

On one wall, near the coloured-chalk order board, three store-bought, dry-mount Art Nouveau posters depict coffee drinkers. The coffee steam rises from the cups, neatly curling into the border design. On the wall behind the counter, five silver and white analog clocks are mounted in a straight line, each with a city name printed in block letters underneath: Tokyo, Los Angeles, Halifax, London, and for reasons not made entirely clear, Beirut. The clocks are wildly incorrect, with their minute hands pointing every which way. The whole effect of the interior design – the bold colouring, the world music, the cleaved scull, and the inaccurate clocks – is mildly disconcerting, as though time and place, culture and politics are just designer off-the-shelf purchases to be interchanged as needed.

Behind the counter, a young woman with brown shoulder-length hair and silver wire-framed glasses smiles. "What can I get you?" she asks.

"A large black coffee, please," I say.

She nods, turns, and grabs a wide-lipped blue mug. She pours black coffee into the mug and places it on the counter. I pay my two dollars then take my cup and my scant change to a seat by the window overlooking the pedestrian mall.

Once seated, I remove from my bag my notebook and newspapers, and rummage in them for the testimony of Matilda Ballard and Sarah Myers. As I do, I recall, for a moment, present-day Artillery Park to the south of Citadel Hill, and recall in particular a red brick building next to the military library. The memory of that structure provides me with a concrete image for the jail that once stood near the Poorhouse. Inside, I imagine Matilda Ballard, upstairs in her cell, sitting at a table. Across the table, staid and serious, still in his overcoat, sits Joseph Howe. He has come to talk with Matilda Ballard again. Ballard has asked him to come this time. She has something she wants to say.

So he comes. And he sits. And he waits, quietly encouraging her. Ballard is reluctant and a long silence fills the shadowy cell, but when the silence becomes intolerable, she looks down at the table and speaks. "I am near twenty years of age," she says, "and I lived five months in Murphy's house." She pauses and sighs. Then she continues, "Sarah Myers, Annie Cole, Jane O'Brien, and myself were the only girls in the house. The men were Murphy, Gordon, and Parsons. As I have told you before, I did not know Alexander Allen. I never saw him before he came to the house on the night he met his death." Ballard looks up into the inquisitive eyes of Joseph Howe, and she begins rapidly telling the story as she remembers it and not as she had crafted it that night.

She says she recalls seeing Alexander Allen and a sailor named Jim Bolden entering the Waterloo around six o'clock. She says they stayed briefly in the taproom, stayed enough time for each to drink a ginger beer. "He treated me to a brandy," recalls Ballard, "and after a quarter of an hour, they left."

"When did Allen return?" asks Howe.

"It was quarter past eleven. I remember because eleven is the hour for closing. I looked at Murphy's watch, which he keeps at the bar. Tom did no more that night than usual. He closed about the same time as he usually did. I think there was dancing that night with some merchant sailors early about five o'clock. But after six or seven o'clock there was no dancing."

Ballard becomes silent again, looking out the window.

After a time, she looks back at Howe and says, "After eleven o'clock Sarah Myers, Dave Parsons, and myself were in the taproom. Mary Cole and Murphy were in his room just off the bar. When Allen came in, his face was cut, with much blood on it. The blood was running over his face, from above the eye. He got two glasses of brandy, drank half one, gave the second one to the black boy, and gave the other glass to Sarah Myers. Sarah asked him how he was hurt. He said, 'Friends on board were enemies on shore.'"

Ballard lets out a harsh laugh, as though Allen's comment had been darkly funny, but then her smile quickly fades, and she becomes silent again.

Joe Howe leans forward, encouraging her to say more.

Ballard complies. "By that time," she says, "Murphy had come to the bar. He told Sarah to take Allen upstairs, and clean him up. She did so, and when she returned five minutes later for some water, we sat for some time together, again, in the taproom. Tom's room door was shut by now, and the bar was down. We could not see the hall or the stairs leading to Sarah's room. That's when I heard some noise, like a rumbling of feet upstairs. I asked Dave Parsons what it was. He said it was up in Jane O'Brien's room. The noise was like scuffling feet. We next heard screeches, which seemed to come from the entry. We ran to the taproom door, leading to the street. It is a door separated in the middle, and one half was opened. And that's when I saw them. I saw Tom Murphy and Gordon dragging Allen down the stairs leading from Sarah's room. The lights were lit on the mantelpiece, and it was light enough to recognize Tom and Gordon – and I know it was the sailor."

Ballard stops talking and raises her hand to her mouth, her eyes filling with tears.

Back in my time-confused coffeehouse, Matilda Ballard's crying is interrupted by two women entering the front door. They are loudly conversing, so loudly that the half-dozen coffeehouse patrons look up. The two women, oblivious to the attention, keep talking as they walk to the counter.

"Can you believe she actually put sausage in the bean soup?" says one incredulously.

"I know, I know," says the other, rolling her eyes and shaking her head, "and she knew I was a vegetarian, too."

The two interrupt their conversation to order. The tall woman, dressed in black jeans, a black sweater, and a black feather-filled vest, orders a double long espresso. The other woman, wearing a rhinestone-filled denim coat and denim skirt with a hint of white lace peeking out at the bottom, orders a caramel macchiato. While the order is being filled, they continue their conversation.

"I'll bet you many people will become vegetarians this year," says the one in the denim skirt. She pauses to push up the scarf that dramatically wraps across her forehead and hangs over her right shoulder. "I mean, once people realize that one and a half tons of CO_2 emissions are saved when you become a vegetarian, they'll change."

"You're so right," says the other, nodding earnestly.

I audibly moan at the inanity of coffeehouse conversation.

Of one famous late-seventeenth-century London coffeehouse – a place called Covent Garden (and Will's Coffeehouse) where poets John Dryden and Alexander Pope, and diarist Samuel Pepys held court – Irish writer Jonathan Swift once wrote, "The worst conversation I ever remember to have heard in my life was that at Will's Coffeehouse, where the wits (as they were called) used formerly to assemble; that is to say, five or six men who had writ plays, or at least prologues, or had share in a miscellany, came thither, and entertained one another with their trifling composures in so important an air, as if they had been the noblest efforts of human nature, or that the fate of kingdoms depended on them."

Some things never change.

The two women take a seat on the other side of the coffeehouse, far enough away that their conversation is lost to me. So, again, I look down at my notebook, and return to Ballard crying at the table with Joe Howe.

Joseph Howe is anxious to hear more, so he gently changes the subject to encourage more talk. He asks Ballard about John Gordon, at which Ballard looks up at Howe. She breathes deeply and her crying stops.

Howe nods his encouragement.

She begins again. "John Gordon had been stopping at Tom Murphy's for about three months," she says. "He was working at McClusky's place next door, often going to Murphy's before he commenced working there. I saw Gordon coming in early in the evening with a bunch of turnips he said he stole. Gordon was there like any other lurcher. I mean by that, that he was getting his bit for nothing. I don't know that he had any connection with any of the women, but I know he never had anything to do with me. Gordon had a particular room reserved for himself."

Howe then deftly returns the conversation to the events in the Waterloo that night. "Tell me again about the taproom."

Ballard nods. "They were dragging him down the stairs, head-first," she says. "Murphy had him by the throat, and Gordon by the waist. Allen was screeching from the time I saw him in the entry until they got him to the bottom of the stairs leading to the street. Anybody in the street must have heard him. His screeches might have been heard a quarter of a mile. The sentry in the Artillery Park could have heard screeches. When they got him down stairs they leaned him up against the wall. There were steps from the wall door and steps from the taproom door, with a little platform between. They set him with his head leaning against the wall. His legs stretched across the platform and not against the banisters. Gordon struck him before he set him down, not after. He struck him with his right hand, as hard as he could. I can't tell what with." Ballard looks Howe in the eyes. "Then they took the man outside. Gordon ran upstairs, took the sash out, and said the man had fallen out the window. Then he walked in the back way and said he would clear out.

"In the tavern, Mary Cole said to Gordon: 'Don't go and leave us in this mess.' Murphy then enters the room from the back way as well – and his hands are full of blood. He points at us and says, 'If you say a word about this, I will take your lives as I did that of the sailor.' Then he turns and walks into his own room. I looked to Mary Cole. And she said, 'My God, what will I do?' I was so scared. 'Don't do anything,' I said, 'or Murphy might serve us the same.' Then Sarah and I then went upstairs to bed, where we lay together on top the blanket, until the watchmen came about half past three."

"Did you see anything else?" asks Howe.

"Yes," says Ballard, "the next morning, I saw Mrs. Ward empty a basin with blood in it out the back door."

In my coffeehouse, I lean back in my chair, sip my coffee, and consider the testimony. At a table near to me, a father and daughter sit quietly together. The father is bald and lightly bearded with a narrow face and weary eyes focused intently on a local newspaper. The young girl, no more than eight, also has a narrow face – much like her father's. She wears two long braids of brown hair that fall in front of a buttoned denim jacket as she leans forward against the table. While her father reads the newspaper, she sips at a bottle of orange juice and diligently writes in a small notebook.

At another table, also close by, a young couple sits. They are dressed in earth tones and matching piercings: in both ears and the lower lip. He wears a black ball cap with brown hair peeking out and long sideburns that reach to his jawline. She wears her hair long and straight. She is a shade too white for good health. They talk about their drinking the night before.

"I shouldn't have gone to that keg party," the young man laments.

She nods and drinks her coffee. The effort seems to take all her energy and focus. "Yeah," she agrees after a silent moment, "me too."

The two sit silently, nursing their coffees.

I return to my notes and to the confession of Sarah Myers.

As he did with Matilda Ballard, Joe Howe sits across a table from Sarah Myers in her cell. Myers, unlike Ballard, is emotionless and cold.

"I am going on twenty-four years of age," she says flatly. "I lived at the Waterloo, kept by Thomas Murphy. I lived there three or four years, but have been in jail since last September." Myers stares for a moment at Howe, who remains impassive. She grins grimly, then continues, "There were Matilda Ballard, Jane O'Brien, Mary Cole, myself, Gordon, Murphy, and Parsons in the house – seven in all. I do recollect the night Allen lost his life. He did not stay long the first time. I saw him in the taproom. When he came at six o'clock, two other sailors were with him. He gave Matilda Ballard a glass of liquor. I saw him standing at the corner when he went out. He went away. I was in the house all the evening." Myers falls silent, waiting for something.

"He came back again, though," prompts Howe.

"Yes," says Myers, "he came in again, about quarter past eleven, about the time the house closed. He was alone, and Murphy was in the bar. Shortis, the fiddler, was there before, but he had gone away by then. I don't think Allen was in liquor, but he did have a cut over one eye, with a little blood on his face. He went to the bar and asked for two glasses of brandy. He gave one to me and the other half to the coloured lad." As Myers continues, she recalls that Allen sat down with her, talking for just a minute or two while she drank the brandy. That was when Murphy asked Allen how he got his eye cut.

"My shipmates have beaten me awfully down in the next street," Myers recalls Allen saying. Myers also remembers that Allen did not appear stupid. In fact, except for the cut, he seemed well.

Then, recalls Myers, Murphy looks to her and says, "Go up and wash the blood off his face."

So Myers takes Allen up to her room and gives him some water. There, Allen sits on a bench in the room and removes his jacket. "My room is over Murphy's," she tells Howe. "I left him there, sitting down on the bench with his hat and shoes still on. Then I came downstairs with the pitcher."

In the kitchen, Myers sees Matilda Ballard by the fire and sits with her to chat. "I got talking to Matilda and did not see or hear anything of Murphy or Cole while sitting at the fire. It was about one quarter of an hour from the time I came down the stairs until I heard the scream. It was not very long. It sounded like a scuffle in the entry. From the time I came downstairs, leaving the sailor in my room, I did not see Murphy's door open, but Murphy could go from his room to mine without my seeing him. I could see nothing of what was doing on the stairs. Gordon was in his own room. I heard him in there, and I did not see him in the taproom. Murphy and Mary Cole were not in the taproom when we went up. The bar was shut. I did not go up again."

"You mentioned the noise," prompts Howe, shifting in his seat.

"Yes," says Myers. "Matilda Ballard and I and the coloured boy were all that were in the taproom then. We heard the noise. The coloured boy said he thought it was in Jane O'Brien's room. We then heard a cry. We went to the door of the taproom, which led to the street. I was standing in the door. Matilda Ballard was with me and the coloured boy. The night was pretty dark. I had left a light on in my room. As I was standing in the door, I saw Murphy and Gordon bring the sailor down the steps. He was not struggling. He seemed to be pretty well gone. When they got down to the bottom of the stairs, Gordon struck the sailor over the head with whatever was in his hand. I did not see Murphy strike him. I saw Gordon go up the same steps, and go in the back way into the taproom. I don't know whether the men saw me. What I saw was the dying man taken down into the street by Murphy and Gordon. They sat him up against the steps. I could not see what the blow was struck with. Gordon used to keep his tools in his room, which was next to mine. The blow he struck the man was on the back of the head. I think it was with a chisel. The blow did knock him down. I saw no blow struck but that one, but I heard the first scream and it sounded as if they came from the stairs, and then a second from the entry. The black boy said he thought the screaming was in Jane O'Brien's room."

"What of Gordon and Murphy?" asks Howe.

"Gordon came up by the south door and went along the back way. He had time enough to go upstairs into my room again, before he came into the taproom. I think he did go up. I do not think that either Murphy or Gordon saw us when they were taking the body down. They might have gone into Murphy's room without returning through the room where we were. After the sailor was down, I went up to my own room again. The light was burning. The door was not pulled to. I had left it open when I came out to get the water. It had a small lock. There was a hasp and staple on it, but these were never used. If there was nobody there, I locked the door and kept the key in my pocket. I positively swear I did not lock the sailor in. When Murphy came in he said that the sailor had taken the sash out and jumped out of the window. His hands were full of blood, and so he passed us. He said if we said anything about it, he would serve us in the same way. I did not see him wash his hands. Mary Cole came out of the room as he went in, and she stood looking out of the door. When he went into the room in that state I saw Mrs. Ward sitting there. When he came out he told the black boy to go with him for the watchmen, and he told me to go to bed with Matilda Ballard, which I did."

Howe asked for more information about Gordon.

"I do not know that Gordon was working for Murphy," says

Myers, "but the house next door was getting repainted, and he was working at it. Gordon went to his room about ten o'clock that night. As I recall, Allen did not come in till after Gordon had gone upstairs. I do not know of any conversation between Gordon and Murphy while Allen was in the taproom. Gordon had his trousers and shoes on when he came down."

In my coffeehouse, I lean back in my chair and consider the second change in testimony. While I do, the young woman who took my order now wipes the empty table next to mine. She looks at my table and sees the mass of papers. She is curious and makes polite conversation.

"What are you working on?" she asks.

"Well," I say, "it's something of a mystery." I then offer a thumbnail sketch of the project.

"Wow," she says, "that's cool." For a brief second I muse that the word 'cool' remains a cutting-edge hip compliment, despite its use generation after generation.

"Are you a student at the Art College?" I ask, putting down my pen.

"I was," she says, "for a semester. I was taking photography, but I couldn't see making a living taking wedding photos every weekend. So now I'm taking courses in business at the community college."

"Cool," I offer playfully, but she either misses or ignores my lame use of the word. Like so many twenty-something people I come across, she relishes the opportunity to talk about herself, and after another prompting question from me, she shares a grand stretch of her life's story.

"I grew up in Lunenburg," she says, "and I spent the first nineteen years of my life there. I am twenty now." She says she's 'twenty now' in a way that suggests the crossing of a great divide, from childhood to adulthood. "I came to Halifax to study, but, really, I want to travel. I even changed my major to International Business because there is a work term in Thailand." She positively glows at the prospect of seeing faraway lands, at the prospect of escaping the small town world.

"My friends all still live at home," she says with a hint of contempt. "They don't have jobs, and they live with their parents. They're all still stuck in high school." As she talks with great animation, I find myself seeing in her face, the faces of Sarah Myers and Matilda Ballard. I wonder if they too escaped to Halifax from small towns.

The woman talks for a while longer about her enthusiasms for travel, until she realizes that someone is waiting at the counter to order. She finishes her conversation by saying, "But you know, I'm really just a country girl. And I'd like to get a small piece of land back home someday." With that, she turns and walks back to the counter to take an order.

I muse that the words of a twenty-year-old sometimes percolate with unintentional wisdom. She is right. Likely, no matter how far she travels, nor how far she stretches, her roots will always be in small town Lunenburg, Nova Scotia, an enviable connection to the earth that is hard to come by in a Digital Age.

I look back down at my notebook and finish listening to Myers' testimony.

"What happened next?" Howe asks her.

"I went in my own room and found the sash was out and several panes of glass broken. The sailor's shoes and stockings were lying down. I was frightened to take them down into the taproom and dropped them out the open window into the street. Before I went upstairs, Murphy had gone away and Gordon said he was going to clear out. Mary Cole told him not to go away and leave her in that mess. I threw all his things out of the window. I did not know what to do with them. No person spoke to me from the street below when I was chucking out the things, nor was any girl looking out of the window above me. I threw the sailor's clothes out. I hardly know why. After throwing the things out, I went back to Matilda Ballard's room and was there till the police came for us."

"Are you aware of any threats issued by Murphy against Allen?" asks Howe.

"No. I never heard Murphy use any threats about Allen," Myers answers.

"Why didn't you give this testimony earlier?" asks Howe.

"I was taken into custody about three o'clock in the morning and the next day examined before a coroner's jury. I did not disclose what I now do, because I was afraid of Murphy. But then, I thought it best to tell the truth." She looks pleadingly at Howe, showing the first real sign of emotion. "My sole reason for secreting this evidence at first was fear of Murphy."

I consider that the stories of Myers and Ballard are plausible enough. In any crime, motive, means, and opportunity are necessary elements for conviction. Certainly, Murphy had all three. Gordon, however, remains more mysterious, somehow working for Murphy, somehow his accomplice.

Thumbing through my newspapers, I note that on December 15, 1853, two months after the mysterious death of Alexander Allen, a partial eclipse obscured the sun. Perhaps Matilda Ballard and Sarah Myers, jailed as they were, did not see it. But I wonder: if they had, would they have interpreted it, as with the meteor, as another dark omen?

If they didn't, perhaps they should have.

Even after all the evidence is examined, and with nearly all the testimony heard, the mystery is no closer to being solved. As I pack my bag and leave the coffeehouse, heading up Duke Street toward home, I consider that trial of Thomas Murphy, John Gordon, Mary Anne Cole, and David Parsons is all that remains to be heard. I consider that, perhaps, at the trial, the truth will finally emerge, and my mystery will give way to justice.

Yet, in the end, in nothing less than the hands of Justice Thomas Chandler Haliburton, my justice would only give way to more mystery.

Chapter 10

The Trial

"Justice," wrote eighteenth-century essayist Edmund Burke, "is itself the great standing policy of civil society; and any eminent departure from it, under any circumstances, lies under the suspicion of being no policy at all." Of course, when Burke penned these words in 1790, justice, as often as not, meant getting one's ear lopped off as a 'civilized' response to petty crime.

Still, despite the eighteenth century's predilection to van Gogh-style justice, Burke makes a worthy point, one that I consider on a cloudy, cool morning, walking south along Hollis Street, just past George Street. I am heading toward the gates of Province House, the seat of government in Nova Scotia since 1819. In fact, my musings on 'justice' are born of my trek to Province House, since it was here, in late April of 1854, that the Nova Scotia Supreme Court tried Thomas Murphy, John Gordon, David Parsons, and Mary Anne Cole for the murder of Alexander Allen.

I am particularly enthusiastic about this trek into the past because Province House contains the only room I know of where all the people involved in "this most mysterious affair" sat in a wooden witness's chair next to a judge's bench and told their dark tales about death at the Waterloo Tavern – except, of course, for Alexander Allen.

As I reach the gates of Province House, I recall that, for Nova Scotians, medieval justice gave way to modern justice some fifty years after Burke penned his musings – in March of 1841 – when a legislative act entitled "An Act to abolish the punishment of Pillory, Cutting the Ears off Offenders, and Whipping, and to substitute Imprisonment in lieu thereof" was delivered to the people of Nova Scotia.

The act reads like a summary dismissal of medieval inquisitors: "Be it enacted by the Lieutenant-Governor, Council and Assembly, that, from and after the passing of this Act, judgment or sentence shall not be given and awarded against any person or persons convicted of any offence whatsoever, that such person or persons do suffer the punishment of being set in the Pillory, or of having his or their ears nailed thereto, or cut off, or do suffer the punishment of being whipped – any Law, Statute or usage to the contrary notwithstanding. And be it enacted that in all cases where the punishment of being set in the Pillory, or of having the offender's ears nailed to the Pillory, or cut off, or of being publicly or privately whipped, has hitherto formed the whole or part of the judgment or sentence to be pronounced, or has in any other case been inflicted, it shall and may be lawful for the Court, before whom any such offender shall be tried or convicted, to pass sentence of imprisonment, or imprisonment with hard labour, in the Common Gaol, Bridewell or House of Correction, in the County where such conviction shall take place, or in any Public Penitentiary, Bridewell or House of Correction, which may be hereafter established in any part of this Province; and also, to direct that the offender shall be kept in solitary confinement for any portion or portions of such imprisonment, or of such imprisonment with hard labour – such solitary confinement not exceeding one month at any one time, and not exceeding three months in any one year, as to the Court, in its discretion, shall seem meet."

Of course, justice for the accused at this trial – even in the enlightened aftermath of this act – might well have meant hanging. But justice, in place of mystery, is what I am seeking.

So I eagerly step through the wrought-iron gates, glancing right as I do, past the near corner of the building, to the sizable bronze statue of Joseph Howe – carved, cast, and dedicated in 1904 on the one hundredth anniversary of his birth. The statue's left arm is bent at the elbow, and the right arm is outstretched with the palm forward and open. The face is frozen in solemn features, perhaps caught in a moment of great oratory. The statue is well placed here, for it was Joseph Howe, after all, who brought responsible government to Nova Scotia – the first in the British Empire, in fact, outside of Britain – and the first to bring freedom of speech to the would-be nation of Canada. He did all this, and much more, within the walls of this very building.

I look at Province House with some care as I make my way toward the stairs, having read somewhere that this building is an "exceptional example" of the "symmetrical Palladian style," which to my eyes seems something like architecture for the obsessive-compulsive: every post and pillar, every window and doorframe is perfectly balanced with another post and pillar, and another window and doorframe. Charles Dickens once said of the place, "It was like looking at Westminster through the wrong end of the telescope."

Well, maybe.

More accurately – and I say this from some experience – it's like looking at Westminster through the wrong end of a beer glass. Still, Province House is architecturally noteworthy, standing like the old statue of Joe Howe, somber and solemn, in the heart of this rowdy garrison town, an ironic, perhaps gently comic, expression of British Empire civility among rum-soaked taverns and oft-visited bordellos.

At the top of the stone stairs, I open the antique double doors and immediately find myself confronted by postmodern security. A thin, stern-faced commissionaire with short grey hair and a tightly groomed mustache greets me with a weak smile and a menacing, magnetic wand. He promptly orders me to empty my pockets. So I place my collection of silver coins, a key ring, a black pen, and a black notebook into a blue plastic tray, which I push along a rolling track into a trunk-sized x-ray machine, where it disappears. While my personal belongings are soundly irradiated, I step gingerly though a metal detector trellis, managing not to set off any alarms. Still, once on the other side, I am coldly instructed to raise my arms and receive a thorough going-over by the menacing, magnetic wand. After my scanning, the commissionaire appears satisfied that I am not harbouring concealed weapons or homemade incendiary devices. He curtly nods at the disgorged plastic tray at the opposite end of the x-ray machine. I quickly gather my goods before the magnetic wand gets put to more creative uses. Then I make my way into the centre hall on the ground floor.

To my right and left are rooms for the press and the commissionaires, a lounge for Members of the Legislative Assembly, and the Office of the Clerk all behind closed doors. I have been told that in a number of these rooms there sit a series of carved falcons – all conspicuously headless. Tradition says that sometime in the 1840s, fuelled by an anti-American tirade, an addled, and most likely intoxicated, member of the Nova Scotia Legislature apparently confused the stone falcons for bald eagles – an understandable error for any drunken legislator with no formal training in ornithology – and ran about the room, waving his cane above his head, ranting wildly about the uncivilized Americans, and decapitated the unsuspecting and unfortunate stone birds. It strikes me that the level of debate in this legislative building has rarely risen above the drunken decapitation of falcons confused for eagles – literally or metaphorically. Then again, these same folks did happily approve of nailing ears to pillories as a punishment for crimes until 1841.

Such is politics in Nova Scotia, I suppose.

In another room on the ground floor, someone has created an ode to Joseph Howe replete with colourful display boards and historic photographs. As well, and bizarrely, there stands in the back corner of the room a wooden board where the camera-happy tourist looking for the perfect family photo can place a child's or wife's or husband's face through an oval hole under which is painted Joe Howe's body. I suppose the photo opportunity is someone's idea of Joe Howe as Everyman. I momentarily flirt with the idea of asking the thin, stern-faced commissionaire to come and take my picture as Joe Howe, but then I remember the magnetic wand.

I finish my quick walkabout tour of the ground floor and stroll up the centre staircase into the hall on the second floor. Here, the formal Red Chamber opens on my left. With fluted columns, richly designed moldings, three ornate chandeliers, and a thick wall-to-wall red carpet, the Red Chamber boasts two ornate chairs sitting on a riser at one end of the room for formal occasions. It all suggests much about Nova Scotia's Victorian past. At the other end of the hall resides the Legislative Assembly. When the building was first erected, this room – in proper obsessive-compulsive Palladian Style – mirrored the dimensions of the Red Chamber. However, after a series of changes between 1840 and 1886, the room was crafted into a horseshoe shape, to accommodate offices and a visitors' gallery. Inside the horseshoe, the desks of the Legislative Members face each other across a narrow aisle. At the far end, the Speaker of the House sits, flanked by two massive paintings. One painting – no surprise – is of old Joe Howe, seemingly omnipresent. Both the Legislative Assembly and the Red Chamber are inviting spaces, but I am most interested in the more modest third room on this floor, the room just across from the centre stairs – the Legislative Library.

Through an unassuming low door, I enter a rectangular room about sixty feet from side to side and about thirty-five feet from the door to the windowed wall opposite. The walls, on all sides, are filled, from floor to ceiling – even around the windows – with books, reports, and studies. In the centre of the room are arranged three tables. Two are made of dark wood with drawers and an inlaid leather surface. Around each are placed six wooden chairs. The third table is square with a wooden top and is also circled by six chairs.

As I enter, I see the librarian's desk by the south wall to my right. Behind it, a woman sits erect, typing on an old desktop computer. She appears every bit the librarian with short, grey hair tied behind her head and keen eyes behind wire-framed glasses that say, "We will have no silliness here." She looks me over as I enter and quickly determines that I am mostly harmless. She nods and returns to her computer screen. Taking the nod as approval to enter, I walk to one of the leather-topped tables and remove my coat.

"Wasn't this room the Supreme Court of Nova Scotia before 1862?" I offer to the librarian as conversation.

"Why yes, yes it was," she says, looking up and smiling. "In fact," she says proudly, "my desk sits where the judge's bench would have been." With a little prompting, she begins describing the room as it once looked when it was the Supreme Court. Without breaking eye contact, I pull out a chair at the first table, place my notebook and pen on the leather top, and take a seat. While she speaks, I find myself imagining the room in April of 1854.

By mid-morning, on Friday, April 21, 1854, a group of twenty or so citizens and reporters have gathered outside the doors of the Legislative building. The mood is surprisingly light. The group chats with guilty anticipation of salacious tales to be told inside. Just before ten o'clock, the doors open, and the group enters the ground floor. They climb the centre stairs to the second floor and walk across the hall to the wooden door of the Supreme Court. The single guard allows them in to the room, one after the other. They turn left, walk to the back corner of the room, and climb a short staircase to a balcony that overlooks the court.

Already sitting below, opposite the balcony and near to the windows, are the accused – Thomas Murphy, John Gordon, Mary Anne Cole, and David Parsons – all on trial for the murder of Alexander Allen. Opposite the accused, the jury sits in a small wooden jury's box tucked against the wall. Between the accused and the jury box, the simple wooden judge's bench waits for Justice Thomas Chandler Haliburton.

At ten o'clock sharp, the room becomes silent as Justice Haliburton enters from a small office door in the southeast corner. Along with Joseph Howe, Justice Haliburton may well be Nova Scotia's most famous son. Born in Windsor, Nova Scotia, in 1796, he had done much with his life – a lawyer, a politician, a writer, a judge. He was a member of the legislature in this building from 1826 to 1829, when he wrote his *History of Nova Scotia*. In the 1830s, Haliburton wrote the satirical tales of Sam Slick, printed by Joseph Howe. In fact, as a writer, Haliburton was, in his day, as famous as Charles Dickens. In 1841, he was appointed a Judge of the Nova Scotia Supreme Court. He retired in 1856, travelled to England to live for nearly a decade more, and then died in England, in 1865, in the same year and in the same place as another famous Nova Scotian – steamship magnate Samuel Cunard. But in the courtroom that day, he takes his seat with the confidence born of years on the bench.

Justice Haliburton calls the trial to order.

The court officer stands and reads the indictment. A press member, watching from the balcony, looks at the faces of the accused. He records in his notebook that, among the prisoners seated, only one seems "at all affected" – Mary Anne Cole. She "exhibits the effect of her long confinement," the reporter notes. Her skin has a "pallid hue" and her face a "care worn expression." The others, he notes, sit expressionless, emotionless.

Once the court officer finishes reading the indictment, the trial begins.

From his table, the Attorney General, William Young, stands. His chair scrapes loudly on the wooden floor as he adjusts his robe hung neatly over a tailored suit. He nods at the judge. "If your Lordship pleases," he says.

Justice Haliburton nods in response.

The Attorney General then turns to the jury. "Gentlemen of the jury, you will observe from the indictment which has just been read to you that Thomas Murphy and John Gordon have been charged with the commission of the grave and serious crime of murder and that the other two prisoners at the bar – David Parsons and Mary Anne Cole – are accessories after the fact." As the Attorney General calls the accused by name he points with an open hand, palm up.

"The meaning and extent of that charge I shall explain to you before I close," he continues, "confining myself at present to a succinct detail of the facts which I am instructed will be proven on the part of the prosecution. In this indictment the nature of the charge has been varied. But the main question for your consideration today is whether Thomas Murphy and John Gordon did or did not kill and murder Alexander Allen, it not being necessary to allege the particular manner in which the crime was committed, if committed it was."

The eloquence of the opening statement enthralls the courtroom. All are silent. "My object is not to reason much," the Attorney General says, "if at all on the effect of the evidence, which will be adduced, but to open you to the leading features and characters of the testimony, not to influence your judgment, but enlighten your understanding. Of the issue by a detail of the circumstances from which your conclusion of guilt or innocence of the prisoners at the bar is to be deduced. Addressing such a jury as I see now before me I need not ask your grave, calm and impartial attention whilst I fulfill the duty imposed by my public position. There are certain facts in this unhappy case, which, I take it, will not be controverted; others on which we may expect to have conflicting testimony. As you are aware, gentlemen, every case is surrounded with some peculiar circumstances distinguishing it from all others. There are peculiarities in this, which will demand of you serious and calm investigation. But I doubt not that you will deal with these according to those wise and wholesome rules, which our ancestors and the Legislature have laid down for your guidance.

"About midnight of the 7th September last, an unfortunate seaman named Alexander Allen lost his life. By the current testimony of all who knew him it will appear that he was universally acceptable to his messmates – of a quiet, peaceable, and obliging disposition. He came on shore between the hours of six and seven o'clock and the first trace we have of him brings us to the House of Samuel Young – whither, it seems, he had gone on a quest of a woman called Margaret Murphy –" the Attorney General turns and faces the defendants, saying with a dramatic flourish, "the reputed wife of Thomas Murphy, one of the prisoners and from whom he had been separated for some years." The Attorney General then turns to the jury.

"Allen found her at Young's in conversation with a shipmate of his – called Lawrie. I am sorry, gentlemen, to tell you that the house in which she resided was not of good repute and that this trial will reveal a scene from which, it is true, few communities like this are exempt, but which, when brought distinctly and vividly before us, pain and shock the moral sense of every right thinking man. A dispute arose between Allen and Lawrie in the street outside Young's door and a tussle ensued. Allen received a wound on the brow – represented to be a mere scratch or abrasion of the skin followed by an effusion of blood. They parted, however, on good terms, and we next find Allen at Thomas Murphy's – who was the keeper of a house of ill fame.

"It is not my duty, gentlemen, to dwell upon this, to excite prejudice or inflame feeling, but I am required to lay before you every fact within my knowledge that you may judge rightly with all the circumstances under your immediate purview. That house is called the Waterloo Tavern and is situated thus: ascending from the middle of the parade you proceed upward until you reach the street below the Town Clock called Barrack Street, and turning to the left proceeding about halfway between that point and the next street to the south. There stands the building referred to.

"Allen entered it in company with a comrade of his, but nothing material seems to have occurred at this first visit. He went away and again returned about eleven o'clock – the exact hour we may not be able to determine. At that time the following persons were in the house: Thomas Murphy, John Gordon, David Parsons, Mary Anne Cole, Sarah Myers, Matilda Ballard, and Jane O'Brien. These four women were kept there for the purposes of prostitution. So far as I am at present instructed there were no other persons male or female in that house with the exception of Allen.

"Such then was the position of these parties at eleven o'clock on the night of the 7th September last. It appears unhappily for Allen that he had agreed to spend the night in company with Sarah Myers, who will be produced as a witness on the part of the Crown. My object, gentlemen, is not the conviction of these prisoners. Nay, I should rejoice at their acquittal – if it appear to be consistent with the rules of law and evidence and the duty we owe to society."

In the Provincial Library, I am still seated at the table as the librarian finishes her animated description of the room as it was 150 years ago. I thank her. She smiles and returns to her work. So I stand, leave my coat and notebook at the table, and slowly walk about the space, breathing in its history.

It was in this room that Joseph Howe, on trial for libel, made his impassioned defense of free speech. A tarnished bronze plaque in the doorway marks the occasion: "In this room," it reads, "on March 2, 1835, Joseph Howe, publisher of the weekly newspaper *The Nova Scotian*, defended himself in an action for criminal libel. His masterly defence not only won him a triumphant acquittal, but established, forever, the freedom of the press in this country."

I note that, somehow, the modesty of the room doesn't quite fit the heroics of its history. In fact, the room presents itself as an over-filled attic. Along the near wall, on the west side, two wrought-iron and hardwood staircases lead to a narrow balcony that covers three quarters of the room. Two large oil paintings – of Malachy Salter and Susan Salter, prominent citizens in the early years of the city – hang precariously, just over the head of the librarian, from the metal balcony railings. To the left of the paintings, just above a doorway to the small office on the southeast side of the room, hangs a gold scale of justice. When I ask the librarian about it, she tells me that the scale was given to the legislature by a German visitor. As the librarian explains, it has no historic or monetary value. It was only kept because no one wanted to offend the German visitor. So there it was hung.

How very Nova Scotian.

On the recessed window casings, in no particular order or height, and for no particular reason that I can discern, there hang a series of pen and ink pictures and maps. I take notice of two specific drawings of Joseph Howe, one as a young man and one as an older man. Both are offered without date or explanation. In front of one window sits a card catalogue cabinet, despite the fact that a computer for just this purpose is placed nearby. Next to the cabinet stand shelves holding current small-town provincial newspapers.

As I take stock of the room, and make note of some of the oddments, I see small ledges at the ends of the bookshelves. On each rests a small granite bust that – as I am later told – were on display at the famous 1851 Crystal Palace Industrial Exhibition in London. The busts include Queen Victoria, Prince Albert, Prince Edward, British Prime Minister Lord Palmerston, and William Shakespeare. As well, three forearm-size statues of former Prime Ministers

Sir Charles Tupper, Alexander McKenzie, and Sir John A. Macdonald stand crowded together on a dusty windowsill. In front of these statues, on another small cabinet, is perched a small, wooden desktop clock that loudly chimes the quarter hour. To complete the eclectic grouping, an odd, empty, octagonal, wooden umbrella stand occupies the space by the door. This collection of stuff is like that of an elderly aunt's; she can't quite throw anything away, and she isn't quite sure where to put it.

Dizzy from surveying the room, I gather my notebook and climb the stairs to the narrow balcony. At the top, I walk around the corner, with rows of books on my left and the sharp drop to the floor on my right, until I reach the end, where a plain wooden chair overlooks the room. There I sit, pull out newspapers from inside my notebook, and continue to imagine the courtroom in action.

"It is a fact, gentlemen," continues the Attorney General, "that this man in the vigour of his life and youth ascended to the room of Sarah Myers between the hours of eleven and twelve o'clock, that he was sober and in his right mind, that he had a quarrel or altercation previously with Murphy and that of an hour after retiring to that room he is found stretched in the position I have described – a corpse.

"An alarm is given that had he had leaped out of the window, moved by what impulse, actuated by what motive, none can tell. I shall not reason upon these facts. You will have them from the mouths of the witnesses and can draw your own conclusions. The lower sash is found to have been deliberately taken out and one or more panes of glass broken. The balustrade leading up the outside stairs was weak. The slightest concussion would have snapped it. But it remained entirely uninjured.

"Here is one circumstance favourable to the prisoner Murphy. He immediately went for the watchmen – John Shehan and Maurice Power – who had that beat under their charge. Dr. Allan was also sent for – and the City Clerk – all witnesses will be called. And I have only to regret, gentlemen, that the body of the deceased had been moved before Dr. Allan saw it. That body was taken to the Police Office. The coroner's inquest was held and the committal of the prisoners at the bar followed with the other two women.

"About five or six weeks afterwards, these two women voluntarily, as I am informed, and without any inducement or promise of which I am cognizant made a most frightful and startling disclosure. Sarah Myers and Matilda Ballard will be called before you. They will state that a short time after the former returned from the bedroom to the taproom, they were alarmed by screeches coming they knew not whence, that they immediately threw open the door and saw Allen in the hands of Murphy and Gordon, who were dragging him down the stair – Allen's strength appearing to be exhausted.

"When they got him to the foot of the stairs, these girls saw Gordon inflict a wound on Allen's head with some instrument, what they cannot tell. That Gordon then returned into the house by the southern stairs and then Tom Murphy, his hands dripping with blood, came up the northern stair and retreated into his own room into which his mother, Mrs. Ward, by some means unknown to them had gone. The two girls then retired to the room of Matilda Ballard and looking out of the window saw Allen with his head resting on the steps. This testimony was rightfully laid by my predecessor in the office before the Grand Jury and upon it with other evidence the bill of indictment read to you presented.

"I may say to you, gentlemen, that although the character of these women may not be all we could wish, yet I cannot concede nor do I think it will be urged that they are incompetent witnesses and entirely to be discredited. They do not stand in the position of persons concerned in the murder, but if they did, nothing is more familiar to the Law of England than this that the evidence of the accomplice is admissible, although corroborating testimony is generally necessary. These women, however, do not stand in the position of accomplices or approvers.

"But, gentlemen, after the Coroner's inquest was held, after the indictment was found, it came to the knowledge of the late Attorney General that a man resident in Douglas could give material testimony in this case. On the 7th of September last he was living at

Blois' Country Market, and he will tell you something like this: he had occasion to visit a shop at the north end of town and as it was a shortcut he returned through Barrack Street and that, by an almost providential circumstance, just at the instant he was passing the Waterloo Tavern, a little past twelve o'clock, while walking on the western side of that street, he saw two men shoving or jostling or throwing a dead man out of the house and down the stairs. If that be true — and it is for you so to determine what weight you will give to the testimony — there is an end to the story of the man having jumped out the window.

"There are two material questions, gentlemen, which, under his Lordship's discretion, you will have to find. First, has a murder been committed, or did Allen come to his death through his own actions? Second, if murdered, by whom? As for accessories, I am instructed by my predecessor that they were so charged at the insistence of the Grand Jury, who refused to find the bill in any other way, and the extent of their offence will be detailed to you by the witnesses."

Sitting in the balcony, I imagine the Attorney General standing at his table, gathering his notes, and calling his witnesses. He asks them questions; the defense lawyers cross-examine them. I hear the sailors, James Baldwin and William Giles, testify first; then Samuel Young, who keeps a shop on Albemarle and who witnesses the fight with Peter Lawrie; and William Newcomb, the city resident, who attests to Allen's fight with Peter Lawrie; the jailor, James Wilson, who testifies about his interactions with the accused; Peter Lawrie, who tells his tale of fighting with Allen and casts his aspersions on Thomas Murphy; the sailor, Anthony Bambridge, who shares his loyalty to Allen and his memories of that night; the City Clerk James Clarke, who testifies to the scene in the Police Office and at the Waterloo; and Dr. Allan who, in minute detail, tells of Allen's autopsy at the "death house." So too, John Shehan, Maurice Power and Patrick Caulfield, the watchmen and the policeman, tell their tales of that night. They in turn are followed by other citizens and tavern-keepers who provide support for stories told.

I continue imagining the comings and goings of the witnesses as the morning gives way to the afternoon. The jury attentively watches and listens. The balcony crowd occasionally gasps and laughs. After a time, I grow uncomfortable in my wooden chair, so I stand and head down the stairs to the main library floor, where I look for a moment at the small bust of William Shakespeare. Again, I am reminded that the bust is from the 1851 Crystal Palace Industrial Exhibition in London, an event intended to showcase British modernity – industrial and progressive. These small gifts to Province House from that exhibition may well have helped inspire Halifax's own Industrial Exhibition in the fall of 1854. As with London's, Halifax's exhibition – held on the grounds of Province House – was designed to showcase a modern, progressive Nova Scotia, designed to speak to its industrial future.

Some months earlier, while looking through historical documents on the third floor of the Nova Scotia Archives, I came across a thick, twelve-inch by eight-inch, black leather notebook. Between its covers, in neat penmanship on lined paper, handwritten entries were scrawled for the 1854 Industrial Exhibition. The entry list, running for pages, was expansive: eighty-two displays of the mineral kingdom, a variety of local grasses, 167 displays of grains, sixty-five displays of fruit, 359 displays of roots and cabbages, 172 displays of seeds and flowers; so too there were thirteen fat cattle, seventy-two working oxen and bulls, sixty-three cows and heifers, ninety-seven horses, seventy-eight sheep and rams, twenty-two swine, and sixty-three displays of poultry; sixty manufacturers in metal were shown, 141 manufacturers in wood, seventy-seven displays of grain, 117 parts of animals, and eighteen displays of fish; as well there were 164 displays of fine arts, twenty-one displays of literature, forty-six displays of models, and eight displays under the heading of miscellaneous; and finally, there were twenty-eight displays of Indian Work, 223 displays of fine arts in the Ladies Department, and ten displays of music.

A contemporary drawing of the event shows flags waving over the building and tents erected on the grounds, while crowds walk the streets in their best clothes. The irony of the exhibition is striking. Despite the intention to showcase the industrial future of Nova

Scotia, the mostly agricultural displays of the Industrial Exhibition of 1854 underscore how the Industrial Age had yet to take root – and never truly would.

I walk away from the bust of William Shakespeare and make my way to the right of the entrance doorway, to a small alcove among the bookshelves. There, I sit in an upholstered wooden chair covered in red fabric. Likely it was in this spot that the jury sat. From their perspective, I imagine the trial still unfolding.

The Attorney General invites to the stand another witness, an older man with weary eyes and tussled hair. He takes his seat and is sworn in. Then the Attorney General asks him his name.

"My name is Richard Powell, and I live at Douglas about forty-seven miles from Halifax," he says. "I have been subpoenaed to appear here."

"Do you know the accused?" asks the Attorney General.

"Well, I know Thomas Murphy," Powell says. "That is to say, I saw him at the Police Office. But other than him, all the prisoners are strangers to me, and I do not know of seeing Murphy before that."

"Will you share with the court your knowledge of this incident?" asks the Attorney General.

"Well, I was in town in September last, on the 7th. The night was dark as I recall, and I put up at Blois' Market or Steele's. I had a load of produce. I strolled out that evening. I was in Newtown, in a corner shop, near a slaughter house, and left about 12 o'clock. I heard the watchman call the hour as I went along Barrack Street."

"And what did you see there?"

"While I was going past the house Murphy occupied, called the Waterloo, I saw a couple of men come out of a door and throw a man downstairs. And then I heard a cry of 'Murder!'"

"What did you do?"

"I just passed along, and then stopped and returned a piece, but stopped again, for I was afraid to go near."

"Were you able to see the faces of the men?"

"No. I was passing along the western side of the street. I was nearly opposite the house. I could not distinguish which door, north or south, and I do not know who the men were that threw the man out."

"What happened then?"

"The next morning I bought a cow from Mrs. Fox at Fort Massey, and got my breakfast pretty late. A man of the name of Beals went with me to the fish market before breakfast. This was before going to Mrs. Fox's. The fish market was open when I got down, and Beals got his fish. We came up after having a horn of grog at McCarthy's."

A murmur of surprise ripples from the balcony.

"Yes, I see," says the Attorney General. He is anxious to move quickly from the comment, but before he can ask another question, Powell continues.

"I take a horn of grog whenever I can catch it," he says, "and it is none the worse before breakfast." The balcony crowd laughs. Powell smiles, enjoying the attention, then continues his testimony. "At the fish market," he says, "I heard that a man had been murdered, and I mentioned what I had heard the night before. Some people told me to say nothing about it. But still I went into the Police Office and saw the body. Murphy was there. I did not tell him what I saw. I left town that afternoon and did not go before the coroner's inquest because I wanted to keep out of trouble. When I came to town again, the man that came to question me at the market about what I had seen was a shortish man." Powell leans forward and points to the Attorney General: "About the size of the Attorney General there."

The balcony crowd again erupts in a burst of laughter. The face of the Attorney General flushes. Powell smiles at the unintended amusement he has caused. Judge Haliburton quickly orders calm from those present, and the laughter dies away. Powell continues. "Before this, I had got a letter from Mr. Uniacke [the previous Attorney General] and paid no attention to it. Afterwards, I got a subpoena. Then Mr. Uniacke gave me £1 to pay my first expenses. I am a poor man, and not able to live in town on nothing."

"Thank you, Mr. Powell," says the Attorney General.

Mr. Johnston, one of two defense attorneys, then stands and begins his questioning of Mr. Powell. "You mention you 'take a horn of grog when you can get it'?"

"True enough," says Powell.

"How did you know the time when you left the slaughter house?"

"I left a shop there about twelve o'clock. I ascertained from watches in the pockets of people around what time it was."

"How many times, Mr. Powell, did you drink that night?"

"I can't tell how many times I drank. I drink whenever I need it."

The crowd laughs.

"How much do you need?" inquires Mr. Johnston.

"I never keep count of such things when I am travelling," says Powell. "I dare say, Mr. Johnston, you would like a little yourself, if you were on the road." Again, the crowd erupts into peals of laughter, followed again by an admonition of Justice Haliburton.

Mr. Johnston follows up with another question. "If you drank as little as I do in travelling, it would be better for you," he says. "Did you drink three, six, or ten glasses or horns?"

"Maybe not three."

"You say how that you ascertained the time from watches. You say in your direct examination that you heard the watchman call the hour."

"Yes, I heard him. I was never in the Waterloo that I know of. I met a lawyer villain on the Rawdon Road trying to pump out of me that I had been in Murphy's about a year previously. He saw me near the Thompson farm, toward Rawdon. That night, the two men thrust the body out into the walk. I only heard the cry of 'murder' once. I was about two rods distant. All they did was to throw the body out of the door. They did not come down the steps. I did not take particular notice as to which steps the body was thrown over. I did not go near the body. I was about two or two and a half rods from him. He fell into the sidewalk and did not take notice of the stairs. A man passed me about five or six minutes before I saw the body thrown out. He was going the opposite way from me. He had just passed Murphy's house. I don't know how many steps there are to Murphy's door."

"Did you tell a gentlemen a few days ago that there was but one step to Murphy's door?" challenges Johnston.

"I ain't going to say anything about it," responds Powell.

"Was not the impression on your mind when you came to town that there was only one step to the Waterloo?"

"I'm not answering any more about it."

Judge Haliburton grows frustrated by Powell's evasiveness. He interjects, "But we must have no trifling here. These men are on trial for their lives, and you must answer all proper questions."

"Well, Judge," says Powell, "I did not go near the body to see whether he was drunk or not."

"So you answer after all," says Johnston, taking the charge. "Now, did you say to that gentlemen that you would take care the lawyers in Halifax should not get the advantage of you, as they would find all your button holes well stitched?"

"Yes," says Powell looking down at his coat and then up again at Mr. Johnston, "and so they are."

The crowd erupts yet again with laughter.

"Do you recall raising a story to a Mr. Smith about a Mr. Loupe or Luke, being murdered in Rawdon, some years ago?" asks Johnston.

"I dreamed," said Powell, "that I saw his bones somewhere in a certain place, and told Mr. Smith so."

"Didn't you take the whole neighborhood out to see, and frighten all the old women and children in the county?"

"No," says Powell, surprised at the question, "the man who brought you that story was a mischief-maker and had little to do."

"You say you saw someone pass you in the street after you heard the cry of 'murder'?"

"I think the man that passed me on Barrack Street was the watchman."

"And still, with the cry of murder in your ears, you did not call him? You were past the Waterloo door about two rods when the man was thrown out, and then you walked two rods further before you heard the cry of murder."

"Yes."

Mr. Johnston tells Justice Haliburton that he is finished questioning the witness. Richard Powell is then dismissed.

I walk back to the desk in the centre of the room, where the Attorney General rises and calls to the stand Sarah Myers. I sit and imagine her testifying for an hour or more, relating the events of the evening as she related them to Joe Howe in her prison cell. The crowd is rapt with attention. When she finishes, and is then cross-examined, Justice Haliburton calls an end to the day and recesses until the next morning.

I scan the papers for the next day's testimony. When I find it, I note that on Saturday morning, Matilda Ballard testifies as Sarah Myers had, repeating all she had said to Joseph Howe, implicating Thomas Murphy and John Gordon. Finally, the prosecution rests with the testimony of Joseph Howe. I can only imagine the look that may have passed between Justice Haliburton and Joseph Howe as Howe took the stand, two of the most famous sons of Nova Scotia, whose friendship waxed and waned, sitting nearly side by side in this modest room.

A second defense attorney rises from his table. W.Q. Sawyers, lawyer for the accused, nods at Justice Haliburton and turns to the jury. "By permission of his Lordship, I address you, gentlemen, on behalf of the unfortunate persons whose dearest treasure – their lives – are in your hands today. It is my privilege under the law briefly to open to you the testimony, which in our opinion is essential to the case of the prisoner – and in doing so I shall endeavour to keep within the time laid down for our guidance. I may, however, congratulate the prisoners that their case is in the hands of a jury so intelligent and impartial; and myself upon the fact that any deficiencies of mine will be amply supplied by your judgment.

"The testimony we shall offer will be first – Samuel Parker and P. Flynn who we are advised will prove, that when raised from the ground, after having been knocked down by Lawrie before Young's door, Allen appeared stupefied and that his subsequent conduct was such as to induce the belief that he was in an uneasy and unsettled state of mind. We shall next call Dr. Gilpin and Dr. Parker not for the purposes of contradicting Dr. Allan, but to explain certain matters not touched by him, and next to prove the improper manner in which the confessions were extracted from Ballard and Myers – Henry Adams and William Mills will be put upon the stand – and I need hardly say to you that it is our intention to contradict entirely the evidence of Wilson.

"We shall prove the situation of the girls when first incarcerated and the wonderful altercation which took place in the treatment mete out to them after they made the extraordinary statements you have heard from their lips. Jane O'Brien will be called. A girl living in the house at the time of the alleged murder is said to have been committed – whose statements conjoined with those of David Parsons will, I think, conclusively prove to you, that the evidence given by Sarah Myers and Matilda Ballard is not entitled to your consideration in the slightest degree. Of Richard Powell we have heard much; the insolent and flippant and dogged style characteristic of the manner in which his testimony was given must have left its impression on your minds as it certainly did on mine. I am instructed that we shall be able to prove from the mouth of a poor black man called Patterson, living in the City – of respectable character, that he was engaged last December in prosecuting fishing in the Northwest Arm. He recollects the night on which Allen met his death, recollects seeing a man hanging from, and then falling from, a window at the Waterloo Tavern.

"With this brief abstract of the defence; and with the evidence in support of it I shall close – feeling confident that in analyzing these circumstances you will be influenced but by one desire, the attainment of truth and the administration of justice."

After this, the defense lawyer provides a series of character witnesses for John Gordon and Thomas Murphy. He then puts Jane O'Brien on the stand, and she corroborates the testimony of the accused; then comes David Parsons, who remains true to the tale he first told that night in September; and finally, in direct counterpoint to Richard Powell's testimony, the defense puts John Patterson on the stand.

I sit back in my chair and read the testimony with fascination.

"Tell the court your name and why you have been called," says Sawyers.

"I lived, in September last, in a house owned by Samuel Parker," says Patterson. "I came from Terrance Bay, this side of Prospect. I was engaged in some fishing, frequently at night. I remember the night the sailor Allen came to his death. I was coming from the Arm, and I heard to watchman call, 'All's well.' I came in by the Artillery Park, walked through Barrack Street, and, when I got between the Waterloo Tavern and the new building, I heard a noise."

"What was it?" prompts Sawyer.

"I looked up," says Patterson, "and saw a man hanging from the ledge of the window by his hands. As I was moving towards him, he fell. I then heard a noise inside and a man came out and said, 'Good God, the man is dead!' The man returned to the house at once and came back again accompanied by another man. One said to the other, 'You stop here until I go for the watchman.' I then turned back, walked down the south side of the Waterloo Tavern and went home. When I got there the door was locked. The wife was to bed. She got up and let me in."

"Why didn't you come forward with your story earlier?" asks Sawyer.

"I did not go to Murphy and tell him for my wife said I had better have no hand in the matter," answers Patterson. "But when we heard that these girls were going to hang the men, my wife said, 'It was a shame before God and man to have innocent men hung for nothing.' I never related these circumstances to Parker or any one else but to Judge Sawyer. I allowed these persons to remain in jail for six weeks. I heard that they were in jail and knew they would not be released till the Court but that was not the reason why I did not tell. I did not tell because the girls first told the right story, that the man had fallen from the window. And I only came forward when I heard they had contradicted their own testimony and sworn that Gordon and Murphy murdered the man and carried him down the stairs and thrust him out the door. Any one who swears that this was the case lies. If the girls have said so, they have stated a falsehood."

I am dubious about Patterson's testimony. It seems too neat, too contrived for the defense. Besides, in counterpoint, the sum of the other evidence and testimony is weighty, the stories of the defense too riddled with holes and contradictions. Frankly, if means, motive, and opportunity are the three criteria to satisfy guilt – and thus justice – then John Gordon and Thomas Murphy have much to answer for. But as the fiddler, Thomas Shortis, takes the stand, Judge Haliburton abruptly stops the proceedings.

"I would like to know from you, Mr. Attorney General," says Judge Haliburton, "whether, after the very contradictory testimony given, you think it prudent to proceed further with the prosecution. With such evidence before them, I am sure no jury would feel themselves justified in convicting the prisoners. Had it been a week, perhaps I should not have interposed, but the jury will be detained after four days, for perhaps two more and the same result must of necessity ensue."

"I should not have felt myself justified, My Lord," answers the Attorney General, "in expressing the opinion which in common with Your Lordship, I now entertain respecting the case. Clouded with suspicion as the testimony for the prosecution undoubtedly is in consequence of the position for the parties and their acknowledged character, after the direct and deliberate contradiction with which that testimony has met I do not think any jury, under oaths, would be justified in convicting the prisoners."

"What I feel is this," says Judge Haliburton emphatically, "that in a capital case, where the lives of the parties arraigned are at stake upon the testimony so contradictory and conflicting no jury could feel themselves at liberty, and no judge would be authorized under such circumstances in instructing them to convict, much less would any government feel themselves at liberty to carry sentence of death into execution. The Attorney General has conducted this case in a manner highly creditable, neither relaxing that stringent investigation which every case such as this should receive, nor pushing it beyond bounds."

"It would have been more satisfactory, My Lord," says Mr. Johnston, "if some explanations of which we are possessed were made that the public mind might be relieved of certain erroneous impressions which seem now to prevail. In conjunction with this, my Lord, I should like to have urged two good and almost of themselves efficient grounds for acquittal: firstly, the utter absence of motive; and secondly, the want of time to conduct the detailed and unvaried account of the prisoners before the coroner. I entirely agree with Your Lordship that the prisoners are very candid and moderate manner in which he has conducted on the part of the Crown. I take this opportunity of stating this now and should certainly have done so had I an opportunity of addressing the jury."

Judge Haliburton asks the jury to stand. "After an investigation of three days, gentlemen, it has been deemed inexpedient, both by the bench and the prosecuting officers to pursue this case further. We have heard sufficient to satisfy our minds that no conviction can take place; such, I presume, must also be the impression resting on your mind. Whether the unfortunate man Allen met his death by some act of folly or madness of his own or whether his life was taken by the prisoners at the bar or any other persons is enveloped in mystery – so entire and complete that human judgment is baffled. I have therefore to recommend, gentlemen, that you return a verdict of Not Guilty."

In the jury's box, the jury members whisper among themselves. The crowd in the gallery is stunned into silence by the change in events. After a few minutes, the jury announces its acquittal of the prisoners.

Judge Haliburton then addresses the prisoners.

"You, John Gordon and Thomas Murphy, have been indicted by the Grand Inquest of this county for the murder of an unfortunate seaman called Alexander Allen. You have been tried by a jury of your countrymen, and after a three-day investigation – by the concurrence of a number of accidental and fortuitous circumstances – an impression has been removed, which up to a certain point in this case mitigated strongly against you. The evidence is sufficiently clear to have justified a judge putting it to a jury as circumstantial proof of your guilt. To the providential production of certain counter testimony you owe your escape, an escape, which, innocent though you be is certainly a fortunate one. You must bear in mind that there must have been, and that there cannot otherwise than be a prejudice on the mind of any jury, empowered to try you for the commission of an offence so heinous, whether here or in any other portion of the country – against two men: one married, his wife still alive, a mechanic able to earn his own living, who resides in a bawdy house and does not appear even to have paid his board. In what capacity you were there, whether as a bully or a partner, you, yourself, best know. The other, you, Murphy, have degraded yourself below the dignity of manhood to engage in the occupation of a beast.

"Women we know can be so reduced in the social scale – can become such outcasts from society that both sexes close their doors against them, and the destitute of sympathy, regarded not with sorrow – without pity, without aid, without commiseration – their only resort a den of infamy such as you keep; that, or the grave. But that you, a man, an able and strong man, sufficiently educated to read and write living in such a state of infamy – selling liquor to the unfortunates in your dwelling, that your coffers might be filled – seducing those of the other sex to glut their brutality under your roof that you may pocket your unholy gains – can you wonder that the public should regard you with instinctive horror and feel prejudice of the strongest against you?"

Haliburton stares hard at John Gordon. "You, man, with the semblance and shape of a man, for God's sake, return to the prosecution of your trade and live no longer on the bounties of prostitution."

Haliburton turns to Thomas Murphy. "And you, also, formed in God's image, seek an honest calling. Appropriate your house to a better purpose and strive to repair as far as you can, the irreparable injury you have done society.

"And here, I may remark that it is a disgrace to this city that licenses should be granted for the sale of liquors in houses of such character, collecting revenue off the prostitution of the unfortunate female inmates of these dens."

The prisoners are then duly discharged, and the court abruptly adjourned.

Like those in the balcony, and like those citizens who read the account in the newspaper the following day, I am stunned. Certainly, the details of the murder may have been complex, even convoluted, but the evidence had not been fully heard. Surely, justice required a full examination. But in the end, justice was not served, and only mystery remained.

For a time, I sit and stare at the photocopied newspaper, lying open on the leather-topped table in front of me. With no more testimony to read – and the courtroom having been cleared of the crowd, the lawyers, the witnesses, the accused, and Justice Haliburton – I stand, pull on my coat, and gather my notes. With a quick thanks to the librarian, I leave the legislative library and walk across the hall and down the stairs. On the main floor, I pass the stern-faced commissionaire still holding his magnetic wand, and head out the door, down the stairs, and turn right on Hollis Street, losing myself in thoughts about the trial and its ambiguous outcome. I turn left onto Prince Street and walk east toward nothing in particular.

Somewhere, Edmund Burke, who had written so eloquently about justice, also spoke of justice's relationship to mystery. "Cannot I say," he wrote, "... of human laws, that where mystery begins, justice ends?" So I wonder: is this how "this most mysterious affair" is to end – not with justice but with still more mystery?

Perhaps.

Then again, once more finding myself lying by an old tombstone, in another of the city's old graveyards, I discover that justice may well be served in other ways.

Conclusion

The Justice

In the late afternoon of an unusually cold day on the cusp of spring, I sit in a comfortable captain's chair inside a small northern New England tavern established and built in 1779. I've ordered a delightful pint of the tavern's best bitter, which now rests invitingly in a tapered glass on the wooden table in front of me. It's Wednesday, March 22, and the pub is notably quiet – and notably empty, save for a mother and daughter taking a relaxing late lunch of cheese sandwiches, french fries, and sparkling water. A cast-iron woodstove blazes hot to my left, and the afternoon sunlight spills generously through the windows along the wall to my right. The setting, to say the least, is most agreeable. So I sip at my pint, enjoying the quiet atmosphere of calm, letting my thoughts drift aimlessly toward nothing in particular.

About three-quarters of the way through my pint, I sit back in my chair and casually look around the room until my eyes fall upon the wide, forest-green wall opposite me. On it, someone has written, in small, black letters: "There is nothing which has yet been created by man by which so much happiness is produced as by a good tavern." The author of the composition is poet, essayist, and regular English tavern patron, Samuel Johnson. And the date given for his composition is March 21, 1776.

Admittedly, I am taken with the wisdom of Johnson's words but also with the date of his composition: committed to print 230 years – plus a day – from the moment I am sitting, enjoying a pint of the best bitter in a New England tavern nearly as old the quotation itself. As a longtime connoisseur of coincidence, and coincidentally a longtime connoisseur of warm taverns that serve good pints of bitter, I steep for awhile in the idea that this all must mean something terribly important. Yet, in truth, I know that coincidence – like its cousins, happenstance and fortune – is just the inanimate stuff of animate stories, the individual words of the complex tales we tell ourselves.

Still, coincidence does seem to find fertile ground in taverns. Consider what great tales were born in the coincidental jousting between Will Shakespeare and Ben Jonson across an old table in London's Mermaid Tavern; or what surprising, sinuous connections were crafted by James Joyce for his *Ulysses* at the bar of Dublin's Brazen Head Tavern; or even what dark, brooding poetry, born of coincidence, was left unspoken and unwritten by a drunken, and soon dying, Dylan Thomas on the floor of New York City's White Horse Tavern. And so, with my tapered glass of beer nearly empty, I consider that perhaps there is something more to taverns and coincidence and the concurrent birth of story.

That thought remains with me, some months later in downtown Halifax, as I open the door to an Irish pub, situated a block east and south of Province House, at the corner of Prince Street and Bedford Row. The tavern is a spacious offering, laid out in three ground-floor rooms, each three steps up from the last, sprawling through three successive mid-nineteenth-century buildings. The twenty or so tables in the first room are filled with boisterous patrons, all eating, drinking, and chatting. In the far left corner, across from the entrance where I stand, a small, squared stage, replete with accompanying sound equipment and stools, provides an intimate forum for nightly offerings of traditional Celtic music – a varying arrangement of fiddles, flutes, guitars, and bodhrans. On Sunday afternoons, musicians sit around a table near the front and play their jigs and reels old style, for themselves. The dark walls of the room reinforce the Celtic theme, rich with Irish pub trappings – myriad Guinness advertisements, county flags, Celtic knots, and even a letter from the President of Ireland wishing the pub owners well.

With no seats in the offing here, I amble across the room, past the bar, and step up three stairs into the tavern's second room. As I pass through the doorway, I find an empty table by a large, bright window on my immediate right, so I slide onto a cushioned bench, place my bag on the inside, and remove my coat. Just as I get comfortable, a waitress arrives at the table. She is dressed in black from shoulder to shoes.

"What can I get you?" she asks.

I hardly hesitate. "A pint of Rickard's Red."

She nods. "Anything from the kitchen?"

"No thanks."

She turns and walks across the room, also abuzz with a dozen or more patrons eating, drinking, and chatting. As I watch her go, I note more colourful Irish pub paraphernalia on the walls – more Guinness advertisements, a signed football team jersey, a painting of a castle, and more Celtic knots. In the far corner, built into the wall, a television shows a soccer match – Liverpool versus Manchester United. But no one is watching. So I give the game a few minutes of my attention, until my waitress arrives with my pint. She places the glass down on a cardboard coaster in front of me, and I thank her. She nods and heads off to another table.

I turn to my bag and remove my black notebook, photocopied newspapers, and photocopied pictures. I spread them out on the table in no particular order, musing that, from this mishmash of inanimate words and images, I have pieced together a rolling tale of history, mystery, and murder. But still, after all my travels, discoveries, and ponderings, the abrupt dismissal of the murder case has left me questioning: how does my story end? How is justice to be served?

So I take my glass in hand, lean back, and sip. I look out the window to my right to muse silently on taverns and coincidence. Up the street, I can just make out the stone wall and iron fence that surrounds Province House, where the trial took place, and I can even discern the outline of Joseph Howe's statue. Noting Howe's arm extended in passionate oratory, I am reminded that he believed newspapers to be the agents and educators of democracy and responsible government. I look away from the window and glance across the room and note another gentle coincidence: this was once the office of Joe Howe's old newspaper, the *Novascotian*. I imagine the space bustling with reporters and editors assembling the news of the day. What, I wondered, did the newspapers think of the trial and Justice Haliburton's abrupt dismissal?

They were stunned, of course.

I put down my pint, lean forward, and look through my collection of photocopies until I find the newspaper from Sunday, April 28, 1854. In it, the editor writes, "At the request of the presiding Judge, we abstained, pending a verdict, from giving publicly to any portion of the evidence in the late trial for murder. For sufficient reasons we have now to regret that we had respect to this injunction. The silent, sullen indications of dissent and disapprobation manifested by the dense crowd of citizens of every rank of society, present at the abrupt, unaccountable termination of this case, will long be remembered by those who witnessed it. This feeling has not abated, while from day to day we proceed to publish the evidence as taken down by the reporters; they who, not present to hear for themselves, have only read the testimony, we may safely say, will participate in the general sense of the community that the 'prosecution did not break down.'

"It is true that circumstantial evidence should ever be deliberately, thoroughly sifted, and weighted in a well-adjusted balance of probabilities. Nevertheless, it will not be pretended that a chain of circumstantial evidence may be such as to reach absolute certainly.

"Now, we would have these people read over carefully, dispassionately, the whole evidence in the case referred to and render their verdict – 'Guilty or Not Guilty.' What say you, people of Nova Scotia? God forbid the shedding of blood that is innocent. There is no maxim more in accordance with the spirit of our religion than this: 'Better that ninety and nine guilty ones escape than one that is not guilty should suffer.' It is right that the accused should take the benefit of every doubt, and that every syllable of rebutting testimony, according to the credibility of the witnesses should be permitted to weigh in his favour.

"There was a time in our nation when witnesses were not permitted on both sides and the bringing of proof going to invalidate testimony offered by the Crown was deemed to involve the indecorous offence of calling the King a liar. It is not so today. And a prisoner at the bar may prove the Crown to be a false accuser, if he can; but surely not by means of such evidences as that which, in the opinion of Mr. Justice Haliburton, is strong sufficiently 'to break down a prosecution.' We are clearly of the opinion that the extraordinary circumstances attending the termination of the trial, which has called for these remarks present matter for inquiry by the Executive Government.

"It may be doubtful whether, in early ages, the Jury were expected to take cognizance of the facts at all, except so far as living in the neighbourhood of the spot whose crime was committed, or for some other cause of knowledge they might be in possession of the facts at all.

"Theoretically, at least, the members of the jury, in our day, are the only judges of the facts under any circumstances. It is for them, after that serious deliberation, which compares with the solemnity of an oath, to render a verdict; and that justice who interposes an opinion of the court to hasten a verdict, constitutes himself (if the Jury permit the infringement) court and jury rolled into one. If this practice be tolerated society will resolve itself into its first elements, and Lynch Law provide a sort of substitute for substantial Justice.

"That's all," the editorial tersely finishes.

Or was that all?

The night before the trial began, the people of Barrack Street – those who knew the accused and who knew the stories – already assigned their verdict, already designated their justice. "At eleven thirty on Thursday night," the Friday newspaper reports, "the 'Waterloo Tavern,' so celebrated as the scene of the Allen murder, was discovered to be on fire, and with the adjoining premises the property of an orphan, was totally consumed. The former was untenanted, and the fire is ascribed to an incendiary. The adjoining property was in part, we believe, covered by insurance."

I fleetingly imagine the Barrack Street citizens breaking the windows of the Waterloo Tavern; imagine them tossing through the broken panes burning rags soaked in oil; imagine the old wooden building catching and becoming a roaring blaze; and imagine the timbers finally collapsing in on themselves until nothing of the old Waterloo Tavern is left – save for memory. Rough street justice though it may be, the citizens have made clear what they think of the tavern-keeper's tale of a sailor jumping, for no particular reason, to his death from a second-storey window. One hundred and fifty years later, drinking a pint in another tavern, once the site of the *Novascotian* paper, just a block away from the old Supreme Court, and just a half dozen blocks from the old Waterloo Tavern, I am inclined to agree.

Consider the facts.

Did Alexander Allen die by an accident? No evidence is offered to explain why he would have jumped through a second-storey window. And though a fall from the window might produce the injuries described by Dr. Allan, no evidence adequately explains how the body was found nine or more feet away from where the body landed. With so little blood on the ground, it seems unlikely that Allen crawled nine feet before dying. And though the earlier fight with the sailor Peter Lawrie might have produced a serious blow to Allen's head, again, the scant blood at the death scene precludes movement of the body after a supposed jump or fall from the window.

As for death by murder, the evidence is far more compelling. The motive? Murphy's estranged wife had a relationship with Allen, and Murphy was overheard threatening Allen. The opportunity? The sailor, alone upstairs with Gordon – a mysterious figure seemingly in cahoots with Murphy – was vulnerable to attack. And the means? Gordon's tools were readily available – and pointedly deadly. Also, the stories of Sarah Myers and Matilda Ballard, even if embellished, ring true. Finally, the fiery verdict of Barrack Street citizens and the editorial of the newspaper suggest that the truth was ignored.

So what of the dismissal? Why did Justice Haliburton stop the proceedings so abruptly? Two possibilities present themselves: one, Justice Haliburton was, as he indicated, impatient with the changing stories of the women in a serious capital case, and he dismissed the charges for the reasons he stated; and two, Justice Haliburton had some connection to the defendants he wanted protected, or he was intentionally ignoring the testimony provided by the two women because his relationship to Joseph Howe waxed and waned. Yet both explanations are unsatisfactory. Justice Haliburton was a man of notable experience and integrity, qualities that make either possibility appear unlikely. Since he left no record of his reasoning beyond his testimony in court, we can never know for certain. So perhaps there is a third possibility to consider.

I take another sip of my pint and look back out the window. The trial's ambiguous finish may, ironically, speak a more definitive truth about the murder and the mystery than any jury's decision could. The truth of Haliburton's dismissal may be more relevant in historical context. I consider that, for Nova Scotians and Haligonians, the coming age itself was ambiguous, an industrial age that promised much for those idealistic believers, but one that never delivered the prosperity of the Golden Age of Sail. Was it coincidence that, throughout the 150 years of the Industrial Age, the agrarian past of sail and seed sustained the imagination and the hopes of Haligonians and Nova Scotians? Seed and sail – culturally, economically, socially – defined, and continues to define, the people of this city and this province.

Perhaps, then, Justice Haliburton dismissed the case because something about the idealistic future must necessarily dismiss the roughhewn past. Thomas Chandler Haliburton and Samuel Cunard and even Joseph Howe all turned their backs on the world of Barrack Street, turned their backs on these people and their lives and their values, turned their backs on seed and sail, all for some siren's song promise of an industrial age. To them, the guilt or innocence of a people relegated to the Age of Sail past was, in the broadest sense, irrelevant. To them, these people were already sentenced and condemned.

So what then of true justice?

I finish my pint and place the empty glass on the table. I catch the eye of my waitress and gesture for another. I then lean forward and look through the photocopied photographs on the table. Slowly and deliberately, I peruse the pictures of Barrack Street, and of the waterfront, and of the Cheapside Market – all from the 1880s and 1890s. I look at the faces of the people and the sailing ships in the harbour. On one particular photograph, I stop for a long time. It is an older photograph, of the Welsford-Parker Crimean War monument at its dedication in July of 1860.

As I study it, my waitress arrives with my next pint. She takes the spent glass and leaves a full. I look up and thank her, then return to the photograph. Below the picture is a record of the newspaper report of the event. "The afternoon was clear, but uncomfortably warm," it said. "A little after 2 o'clock, the procession formed on the Grand Parade. It consisted of all the Halifax and Dartmouth Volunteer Companies, a large number of the Masonic body, and various public officials. These, paraded by bands of music, marched down Barrington Street to the old cemetery, where detachments of the Regular troops of the garrison were already stationed. The military portion of the assemblage formed a hollow square around the monument, within which ticket holders were admitted. A large assemblage, especially of the fair sex, were present to witness the proceedings; and the gloomy old graveyard for once presented a gay appearance. The ceremonies commenced with prayer by the Rev. John Scott. His Excellency the Lieutenant Governor, Lord Mulgrave then addressed the assemblage at some length and, in concluding, introduced the Rev. George Hill, the orator of the day. Mr. Hill's oration was an able and eloquent effort, and is, we understand, to be printed. Major General Charles Trollope also spoke in his usual popular and humorous style, and Rear Admiral Sir Alexander Milne made a few remarks. A great deal of cheering was done and the proceedings concluded by the Volunteer Artillery under the command of Captain Tremain, firing thirteen minute guns, and by the bands playing and the whole assemblage singing the National Anthem. We find that while the ceremonies were going on, Chase, the clever photographer, succeeded in taking an excellent photographic view of the whole scene, a copy of which we have no doubt many people will hasten to secure, as a memento of the day and the event."

As I look at the photograph, I am reminded of how my journey began, lying between two old tombstones in a cemetery, pondering the years between 1840 and 1860. In turn, I am reminded of one more photograph, tucked somewhere in this pile of words and images in front of me. So I flip through the pages and find the picture – a black and white image of the naval hospital graveyard, the cemetery in which Alexander Allen is buried.

The photo shows a scattering of white and grey tombstones on a rolling hill thick with trees. In the lower left corner of the picture, a small, single-storey building stands guard over the dead. Below the photograph I read, "Naval Cemetery: General View of Cemetery, with *Shannon* monument in right foreground, and Gardner's Lodge of Admiralty House to left; about 1882. Looking south-southeast, from top of Wellington Magazine, toward the Citadel, which is in the distance." I've once before seen a close-up photograph of the *Shannon* monument, a distinctive rectangular monument with a triangular top inside a small iron fence. The monument remembers those sailors who died on the HMS *Shannon* during her engagement with, and the defeat of, the USS *Chesapeake* in June of 1813. I consider the location of the monument and the perspective of the photograph, "looking south-southeast … toward the Citadel, in the distance."

From my bag, I retrieve a map of the city, spreading it out on the table. I drop my finger on Citadel Hill then move it slowly north-northwest until I find a small, squared green space inside a military compound, deep in the city's north end. I scan the area around it, looking for any other suggestions of green space or graveyards, but see nothing. So I decide that my finger rests on the site – about two miles north of where I am sitting, along Barrington Street, coincidentally the same street on which the old city graveyard and the Welsford-Parker Memorial are located.

Again, I sit back against the cushioned bench and pick up my pint. I look through the window at the sandstone building opposite me. The Bank of Nova Scotia building has, on its side, a relief carving of an industrial future: factory wheels and smokestacks. I drink my Rickard's Red, thinking for a long time about graveyards and justice, about taverns and coincidence, about the industrial age and the digital age. When I finish my pint, I place the empty glass on the table and make a decision – my story will end as it began, in a grave-yard. I pack up my things, pay my bill, and head for the door. Out-side, I pull my bag over my shoulder and put my cap on my head, then head off on the last leg of my journey – to find the gravesite of Alexander Allen.

Outside, I note the sky is a cloudless blue and the water in the harbour glass still. I stroll along Bedford Row, passing the Art Deco Dominion Public Building on my right and the Art Gallery of Nova Scotia on my left. Further down, I pass the site of the Cheapside Market, now a parking lot looking over the harbour. I cross George Street, looking up for a moment at the Old Town Clock and walk across the space where the Police Office once stood.

Still further along, again on the right, Historic Properties lies bathed in sunlight. I pass the Morse's Teas building on my left then cut across the street, passing the end of Granville mall. I head north along Barrington Street and enter a stretch of 1960s urban renewal, expressed as a dizzying sprawl of overpasses and cement highways, and abruptly leave behind historic Halifax for postmodern ugliness.

To my right, the city's casino flashes day and night, and to the left, the Scotia Square complex of buildings horrifies the eyes. Along the street, a steady line of cars drones past. In the distance, the Mac-donald Bridge spans the harbour and, to my right, the Naval Yard enters my view, a vast sprawl of industrial-block buildings, smoke-stacks, and grey ships in dock for repairs. On my left, the intimacy of downtown has given way to more high-rise apartment buildings and low-rise public housing, punctuated by billboard after billboard. When I finally pass under the bridge, both sides of the street become Department of National Defense grounds, cordoned off by a chain-link fence topped by barbed wire.

Another five or ten minutes further up the road, on my left, a stretch of grass appears, topped by a wrought-iron fence. I climb the grassy knoll until I come to a hole in a chain-link fence and slip through. I then climb over a broken pine board and find myself in an acre of the past, a nineteenth-century graveyard lost amid soulless buildings of brick and cement.

The naval graveyard today looks little like it did in the photograph – fewer than a dozen trees and perhaps eighty tombstones. Still, to my right, inside a short iron fence, I see the *Shannon* Memorial. The monument is in surprisingly good condition, though time has weathered the engraved letters and rusted the iron fence. After looking at it for a time, I walk a dozen steps beyond the monument and turn left, moving slowly along the western edge of the chain-link fence. The gravestones here are in dismal shape. The lettering on many has been wiped clean by acid rain, or the stones knocked over by time and neglect. On some, I can still make out names – O'Donnell, Hill, Tomlins – which I carefully jot down in my notebook.

As I do this, a military police car slowly pulls up and stops along the street on the other side of the western fence. Two thickset, uniformed officers wearing rakish berets exit the white and red car and approach.

"Excuse me, sir," shouts one, "can you tell me what you are doing in there?"

The temptation to say I have just infiltrated the Canadian Forces Base to claim it in the name of Sweden passes, and – since I am holding a pen in one hand and a notebook in the other – I point out the patently obvious. "Well, I'm looking at the gravestones and taking some notes."

"I can see that," he says, considering my answer for some codified, nefarious plot. "And how, exactly, did you get in there?"

I again let the temptation to answer "helicopter drop" pass, and I sigh. "Well," I say, and point at the far corner of the cemetery, "by walking through that enormous hole in the chain-link fence and then by stepping over that broken stretch of two by six wooden board."

"Didn't you see the signs?" he asks with notable irritation in his voice.

In truth, I didn't see any signs. The hole in the fence was at street level, and the broken board was just a few yards beyond that. Still, given the officer's steely glare, I judge that I shouldn't tempt fate by pointing out the clearly egregious state of security on the base, particularly to two irritated – and notably well-armed – military police officers.

"I guess I missed it," I offer with a smile.

"I guess you did," he snaps. The other officer is looking me over now, scanning the potential dangers of my nylon shoulder bag and my Red Sox ball cap. I realize this is going badly, and though an arrest might make for an interesting finish to my adventure, I am conscious that I don't want to wake up in a windowless Syrian prison answering questions. So I edge closer to the fence, still offering my friendly smile, and explain myself. "Look, I am just here searching for the gravestone of a sailor. He was murdered in Barrack Street in 1853. I'm writing a book."

At the mention of "writing a book," the two officers exchange brief, suspicious glances and then start asking pointed, rapid-fire questions about the book's content – perhaps to see if I am, in fact, invading the base for Sweden. After six or eight questions, however, my answers appear to calm them. And after a few minutes more, the officers clearly decide that I am no immediate apparent threat to the East Coast Canadian Forces and then tell me (inexplicably, to my mind after all that fuss) that I can now look around for awhile – so long as I promise to get permission next time. So with nothing else to say, I thank them, and watch as they climb back into their car and drive off.

Arrest safely averted, I return to examining the gravestones. One after another, I read what I can, but glean little information. I begin to accept that I will not find the gravesite, until I come across a singular wooden cross – the only wooden cross in the cemetery. Perhaps this is the grave of a humble sailor. And it is – just not Alexander Allen's. It belongs to a Joseph Pierce who died in 1862.

About ready to give up, I approach the next stone, a thick, brown rectangular monument with a triangular top, much like the *Shannon* monument. Carved into its south side are the words, "erected by their shipmates, 1853." Then I step around to the east side of the stone and read, "In memory of the undermentioned of the H.M.S. *Cumberland*, who died at Halifax." I take a short breath and read the names beneath: George Turner, James Milton, Thomas Maidment, William Fretley, John Butler – and last – Alexander Allen.

My heart races.

I kneel down in front of the stone and slowly run my fingers across the engraved letters. I muse that this is the first moment, in all my sleuthing about, through the past and the present, through the space shared by the citizens of Barrack Street and Haligonians today, that I have tangibly connected with this story, literally touching the past. I turn and sit on the grass by the side of the gravestone and look out at the Narrows of the harbour. I look at the span of the Macdonald Bridge and at the clear blue afternoon sky. "Few places present so pleasing an aspect as Halifax when viewed from the harbour," Thomas Haliburton wrote in 1829. "Its streets are laid out with regularity, its spires have a picturesque and even magnificent effect, and the trees scattered throughout … give it an appearance softened and refreshing."

After a time, I lay back on the grass, beside the old tombstone, letting the warm sun fall on my face. I think about Alexander Allen, think about his murder and think about the trial. In 1854, as Judge Haliburton dismisses the case against the tavern owner and his mates, Charles Dickens was serializing *Hard Times*, his dark meditation on the ill effects of the industrial age. In science that same year, Yale chemistry professor Benjamin Silliman was distilling petroleum, and Nova Scotian Abraham Pineo Gesner, inventing kerosene oil – truly the life's blood of modern society. In London, England, 10,000 people were dying from an epidemic of cholera, which British doctor John Snow traces back to a single well, a discovery that gives rise to the modern study of epidemiology.

Two years later, in 1856, with the signing of the Treaty of Paris, the Crimean War, which had begun in earnest just weeks after Alexander Allen's death in 1853, comes to a suitably inglorious end. At the peace negotiations, lonely stretches of sand and sea are discussed, debated, and dealt out: the Turks keep Moldavia and Wallachia, but both are promised national assemblies; Moldavia is granted the territory of Bessarabia; Tsar Alexander II and the Turkish Sultan both agree not to build military or naval bases on the coast of the Black Sea; and the small Aland Islands, resting in the Black Sea, are demilitarized.

Of course, as with all wars, the Crimean War itself creates a horrific mess, spilling over with military incompetence and political idiocy. As an unintended hinge of modern war, the conflict sees the introduction of trench warfare and deadly, indiscriminate, blanket artillery fire. As another familiar harbinger of the modern war, an outraged media reports on the grotesquely poor treatment of wounded soldiers by many governments. Such reports inspire Florence Nightingale to champion the defense of improved nursing care. Finally, the Crimean War sees the unnecessary deaths of nearly 300,000 people, including Nova Scotians Major A.F. Welsford and Captain W.B.C.A. Parker.

Pondering the events of those few years, and of the generation living between 1840 and 1860, I consider that, for them, the recent past rarely seemed so quickly like the distant past. For those living after 1860, Alexander Allen would have died on the other side of a great divide. No doubt his life, and the larger life around him of sail and seed, was quickly lost to time and fading memory.

Lying on the grass next to Alexander Allen's tombstone, I think: perhaps the most meaningful justice for Alexander Allen is to encourage his Age of Sail ghost to haunt us all, not for maudlin nostalgia, of course, but rather to provide a deeper understanding of who we were, who we are, and who we should be. And in this respect, I feel hopeful. The people of Halifax have long known that the future is not a better place simply because it is the future – they know it is a better place simply because, by remembering their past, they make it that way.

And with that thought, I breathe deeply, my long journey now completed. I stand and walk across the graveyard, amble down the grassy knoll, and step out onto the sidewalk along Barrington Street.

Then I head south – back into the heart of Halifax.